Information and Communication Technology in Development

Information and Communication Technology in Development

Cases from India

Edited by

SUBHASH BHATNAGAR
ROBERT SCHWARE

Sage Publications
New Delhi/Thousand Oaks/London

First published in 2000 by

Sage Publications India Pvt. Ltd
M-32, Market, Greater Kailash, Part I
New Delhi-110 048

Sage Publications Inc   **Sage Publications Ltd**
2455 Teller Road   6 Bonhill Street
Thousand Oaks, California 91320   London EC2A 4PU

Published by Tejeshwar Singh for Sage Publications India Pvt. Ltd, typeset by Deo Gratis Systems, Chennai, and printed at Chaman Enterprises, Delhi.

Library of Congress Cataloging-in-Publication Data
Information and communication technology in development: cases from India / edited by Subhash Bhatnagar, Robert Schware.
     p. cm.   (cl.)   (pbk.)
     A collection of 17 papers based on presentations given at the Workshop on Information and Communication Technology for Rural Development held at the Indian Institute of Management in March 1999, and funded by the World Bank's Telecommunication and Informatics Thematic Group within the Energy, Mining, Telecommunications and Informatics Dept.
Includes bibliographical references and index.
     1. Information technology—India—Congresses. 2. Telecommunication—India—Congresses. I. Bhatnagar, Subhash C. Ii. Schware, Robert, 1952– III. Workshop on Information and Communication Technology for Rural Development (1999: Indian Institute of Management, Ahmedabad)
HC440.I55 I54   384'.0954—dc21   2000   00–028598

ISBN: 0-7619-9444-0 (US-hb)   81-7036-915-0 (India-hb)
          0-7619-9445-9 (US-pb)   81-7036-916-9 (India-pb)

Sage Production Team: Evelyn George, Paramjeet Arora and Santosh Rawat

Contents

List of Tables and Figures

Preface

The case studies presented in this book spell out various applications of information and communication technology (ICT) that have made a difference in the delivery of services or products in rural areas in India. The aim is to draw lessons from experiences in using ICT for rural development by requesting administrators who have piloted and implemented projects in various sectors in rural areas to describe both the opportunities and challenges in the diffusion of ICT. The book tries to look beyond the hype that accompanies discussions of the role and importance of ICT for rural development, prevalent in industrialized countries as well as in political arenas in India.

A considerable number of ICT applications can be found in India at the district level. These have been implemented and well documented since the 1970s. We were looking for applications where there was much greater contact with citizens at the *taluka* level. As editors, we were presented with a wide range of possible papers for inclusion in the book, from what appeared to be futuristic Internet web publishing to computer laboratories in schools. While we believe that increasing access to the Internet will have an impact on the delivery of social services to rural populations, we were reluctant to involve 'what if' applications still in the design stage. We ensured that the applications had been ongoing for at least six months so that some assessment of the impact could be made. Our call for papers for applications at the *taluka* level meant that we were involved with several sectors, as well as with a wider spectrum of organizations, including NGOs involved in implementations. This would not have been possible had we confined ourselves to the district level, where the National Informatics Centre provides much if not all ICT development and support. Some of the papers were based on pilot projects—health, WARANA, village telephony. We realized that if we confined ourselves to large-scale, successful implementations, we would have missed out on some fascinating emerging applications. Nevertheless, all of the projects have borne some fruit.

Analytically, ICT applications in rural development may be classified as those that: provide decision support to public administrators for improving planning and monitoring of developmental programmes; improve services to citizens and bring in transparency; empower citizens through access to information and knowledge; and help in training to improve the functioning of developmental organizations and expand employment opportunities in rural areas.

Chapter 1 assesses the current impact of ICT on development through the computerization that has taken place at the district level. A framework is also provided for assessing potential impact of ICT by discussing some problems of managerial rural development programmes and suggesting a classification of the emerging ICT applications.

Chapter 2 looks at healthcare workers burdened by demanding data-collection and paperwork responsibilities, which affect the quality of their work and their ability to provide primary healthcare services to the people they serve. An innovative ICT pilot application in Rajasthan substituted manual registers with client data stored on handheld computers, accessible through a variety of icons. The objective was to lessen the paperwork burden and improve data accuracy, thereby empowering the village healthcare worker to provide timely care and information. A case in Maharashtra, in Chapter 3, discusses implementation of a GIS-based Disaster Management Information System, designed to ensure better resource mobilization, faster decision making, cost reduction and effective use of common information that in principal should be shared among departments.

Chapter 4 shows how IT-based machines at milk collection centres are used in cooperatives to measure butterfat content of milk, test the quality of milk and make prompt payments to farmers. This has resulted in the removal of incentives to increase the quantity of milk by adding water, reduced time for payments from 10 days to less than five minutes, and has thus instilled confidence in farmers in the cooperative set-up.

Information and communication technologies are an increasingly important part of the Government of Andhra Pradesh's (AP) efforts to improve the efficiency of its administrative offices and to become more responsive to its citizenry. One of AP's major IT projects was to introduce a transparent system of property valuation which is easily accessible to citizens. The project, called the Computer-aided Administration of Registration Department (CARD), is described in Chapter 5. The difficulties faced in implementing this project, spread over 200 locations in the state, requiring extensive re-engineering of a conventional system within a conservative and traditional government department, provides many useful lessons in managing complex computerization projects designed to benefit the 'common man'. AP is the first state in India to design a statewide computerization programme that will be used in rural areas, namely, at the *mandal* level, the administrative unit above the village-level panchayat[1]. There are 1,124 *mandal*s in the state. A review is provided in Chapter 6 of the computerization programme and its first software application, namely, the issuance of certificates pertaining to landholdings, caste, nativity and income across a common counter, without the current delay of 15 to 20 days. Preliminary results can be established on the basis of a six-month pilot project (Chapter 7) that installed a Computerized Universal Postal System and a Centralized Accounting and Reporting System in three post offices in Andhra Pradesh. The technology is designed for rural environments and has embedded components to avoid failures. The systems handle multiple functions within a postal office, reduce errors and waiting time, and provide transparent transactions.

Excellent examples of empowering citizens through access to information and knowledge are provided in Chapter 8. The 'Honey-Bee' knowledge network used to augment grassroots inventors and overcome language, literacy and localism barriers illustrates how ICT can help empower the knowledge rich but economically poor people. The recently launched Warana Wired Village Project covering 70 villages around the river Warana in Maharashtra is described in Chapter 9. The existing co-operative structure has been used in concert with high speed VSATs to allow Internet access to existing cooperative societies. The project aims to provide agricultural, medical and educational information to villagers by establishing networked 'facilitation booths' in the villages. The high costs of private sector provisioning telephones for individuals in villages and the need for public accessibility is discussed in Chapter 10. A DoT-Inmarsat pilot project that involved installation of village public telephones in rural areas, including the hilly terrain of Jammu and Kashmir and the Northeast is discussed. The project also included call pattern analyses, costs and benefits of the project, and a framework proposed through which appropriate communication technologies can be selected for providing telephony services in rural areas. The use of one-way video and two-way audio teleconferencing interactive networks for education and training are discussed in Chapter 11. The major applications of the network in rural development are primarily for training extension staff from various departments of the state governments. In addition, a large number of women, *panchayati raj* elected officials, primary school teachers and child development workers spread over large distances have been trained. Preliminary results are provided of the Jhabua

Development Communications Project, in which 150 direct reception TV sets were installed in villages in a predominantly tribal district of Madhya Pradesh. An end user perspective of the benefits of the one-way video, two-way audio teleconferencing interactive networks for training rural women managers at SEWA (Self Employed Women's Association) is presented in Chapter 12. The results of recent field tests in rural Gujarat in literacy skill development through 'Same Language Subtitling' of film songs on television are presented in Chapter 14. This simple addition to existing film-song programmes shown on television was found to enhance entertainment for the literate and neo-literate.

The scope for adapting and using ICT to enhance functional capacity and improve employment potential of disabled people is demonstrated in Chapter 13. Despite the potential of this technology, it has not been widely used in India due to cost and language barriers, coupled with unsuccessful attempts of the government to develop speech synthesizers, braille embossers and a talking computer.

Entrepreneurship in electronics and information technology maintenance, repair and user training is discussed in Chapter 15. Nearly two-thirds of the 633 All India Society for Electronics and Computer Technology (AISECT) centres located in rural areas are providing direct employment to technicians and trainers. These centres are emerging as multipurpose focal points for training, data processing, desktop publishing, screen printing, medical electronics, communications and community libraries.

In the 1990s, the Indian IT industry has made significant strides. India exports nearly $2 billion worth of software and Indian organizations collectively spend $5 billion buying IT products and services. Nearly one million people attend short courses in IT offered by private training institutions. The Indian economy is increasingly getting integrated with the global economy and the average citizen has a better view of how governments and private sector organizations in developed countries make use of IT to deliver services. Indian society expects improvements in several aspects of government functioning. With the advent of networking and the ubiquitous Internet, there is hope that IT could be used to accelerate the development process. Many state governments in India are preparing grandiose plans to deploy IT in the state administration to provide better services to citizens. Prominent amongst them is the experiment of the government in AP that has been able to attract international funding to support its vision of IT-led development. Chapter 16 discusses the ambitious agendas for the IT sector, outlined by the national IT taskforce and by various state governments. A comparison is made of the strategies adopted by the governments of Andhra Pradesh, Karnataka, Gujarat, Maharashtra, Tamil Nadu and West Bengal.

Finally, Chapter 17 shows that implementing ICT in rural development projects will require paying attention to three key factors of success, revealed by the pilot studies, namely, for whom, what bundle of services (multipurpose), and how well they are managed. The characteristics of projects obviously vary from problem to problem, even in a given country. But these factors seem to be the realities to which future development programmes, funded by governments and bi- and multilateral agencies, must adjust.

Acknowledgements

For assistance of various kinds in preparing the Workshop on Information and Communication Technology for Rural Development held at the Indian Institute of Management in March, 1999, we are indebted to Gopal Pillai, Nina Musale, Janki Swaminathan and Vivek Gupta. It was the inspiring work of the practitioners invited to speak at the workshop that suggested to us the importance of compiling these cases for presentation to a wider audience of government officials, private sector firms, and bi- and multilateral funding agencies. The World Bank's Telecommunication and Informatics Thematic Group within the energy, mining, telecommunications and informatics department provided financial support for the workshop. Special thanks also to Gayatri Khanna for editorial assistance and Shilpa Kedar for ably supporting us through the preparation of the final manuscript and annotated bibliography. For their special blend of encouragement and inspiration, we would also like to thank Deepti Bhatnagar and Alice Trembour.

PART I

Introduction

1

Information Technology and Development: Foundation and Key Issues

SUBHASH BHATNAGAR

This volume is an attempt to document successful use of ICT for rural development in India so that lessons can be drawn on the type of applications that are likely to create a developmental impact and the efforts that will be necessary to implement such applications. To put the case studies and the lessons that have been drawn in perspective, this chapter traces the history of ICT use for rural development in India. It begins by defining the kinds of activities undertaken by government and non-government agencies that are taken up as a part of the developmental process. It examines some of the problems that implementation of rural developmental programmes have been afflicted with, and argues that ICT applications could overcome some of the weaknesses in implementation. It then goes on to assess the early efforts in ICT use. Finally, the paper proposes a scheme by which to classify ICT applications and identifies the key issues in implementing these applications.

■ Introduction

Rural poverty in India is a complex phenomena and there obviously cannot be one dominant approach for its alleviation. Many experiments in Asian countries seem to have succeeded in alleviating poverty in smaller pockets (clusters of villages). These experiments were concerned with improvements in micro-level planning, effective supply of credit to the poorest of the poor, improved management of government-run poverty alleviation programmes, and the work of some NGOs in building networks of self-help amongst the rural poor. Most succeeded because of grassroots intervention. New policy initiatives taken from time to time have been able to provide greater resources for poverty-oriented programmes, education, health or family welfare.

However, it is widely acknowledged that there is a great deal of waste in the way these resources have been utilized in the past. Information technology (IT) is often identified as a key to improve the resource allocation process and to more efficiently implement programmes. Information and communication technologies (ICT) are indeed generating new possibilities to attack problems of rural poverty, inequality and environmental degradation. Old ways of doing business in terms of delivering important services to citizens are being challenged and sometimes abolished in both industrialized and developing countries. But the question of the value of IT for rural development is accompanied by this dilemma for decision makers and multilateral funding institutions: should the very limited resources for rural development be applied to developing ICT capacities, or are they best used for other high priorities such as schools, hospitals and dispensaries? Clearly, there is grave concern about the possibility of wasted, poorly utilized, or otherwise unspent resources in ICT applications for rural development.

■ Development Programmes and their Implementation

Some of the causes of extreme poverty include inadequate infrastructure such as roads and electricity; inadequate access to government functionaries, health workers, primary school teachers, agricultural extension workers; and poor resource base for productive economic activity. Various programmes and activities have been taken up in order to address these causes, including:

- Provision of basic infrastructure in rural areas, e.g., setting up new schools, health facilities, rural roads, drinking water supply and electrification;
- schemes aimed at promoting rural industry, increasing agricultural productivity and providing rural employment;
- providing productive resources to individual families below the poverty line to increase family income; and
- providing food items at subsidized prices through the public distribution system to shield the poor from price rises.

These programmes are implemented through a vast network of government officials at central, state, district and *taluka* (a sub-unit of the district, of which there are about 5,000 in India) levels. Legislators, political activists, elected representatives and the public are the focal points for creating demands on the administrative system. In recent years, non-profit organizations (NGOs) are also playing a key role in providing social services.

At central and state levels, policies are laid down and resources are allocated. District-level officials representing the middle rung of administration are responsible for micro-level planning and monitoring. Actual implementation of most programmes is done by *taluka*-level officials.

■ Problems in Management of Rural Development Programmes

In spite of substantial expenditures in rural areas during the last 50 years, there are regions which are still backward. A significant proportion of the population continues to live below the poverty line (a minimum subsistence income level used by the Government of India). There are some generic problems which plague public administration in every country (Avgerou 1990; Hooja and Mathur 1991; Paterson 1982). This section discusses these problems in the context of rural development programmes in India.

Centralized Planning

Planning has traditionally been heavily centralized. New programmes for rural areas are planned at the state and central ministries, often without access to a detailed status report. A centrally planned scheme may not be appropriate because there are differences in agro-climatic conditions, skill base of the rural population, access to social infrastructure and literacy levels amongst districts. The Planning Commission (1984) recommended in 1984 that powers to allocate and use resources should be pushed down to district-level agencies, which have a much better feel for local conditions. But, such decentralized planning needs to be supported by regional databases and tools for spatial planning.

Multiplicity of Agencies

A large number of agencies are involved in rural development. Very often several programmes such as adult literacy, family planning and loan assistance through the Integrated Rural Development Programme (IRDP) are aimed at the same beneficiary. Ideally, such programmes would be coordinated at the grassroots level. Many of the services complement each other and a lack of one service affects acceptance of other services. To illustrate, low female literacy and poor immunization diminish acceptance of family planning methods. In India, these services are provided by three different agencies. One solution is to reorganize all associated departments into one unit. This may make the department unwieldy—and in any case, vested interests would not let departments be reorganized. Sharing information across departments can improve coordination and planning.

Bureaucratic and Administrative Problems

Over the years the government agency has not reoriented itself from a regulatory apparatus to a development agency. Because of sheer physical distance of field functionaries from their supervisors, there is corruption and slackness in work. The district collector (head of administration at the district level) has become overburdened and his role politicized. The addition of several new departments and programmes has added to the collector's responsibilities to coordinate amongst departments through committees. A collector may often chair about 60–70 different committees (Roy 1991). The average tenure of a collector in a district is about a year, which leads to a short-term orientation. Decentralization of power to *taluka* levels with effective monitoring from the collector's office could help lessen clerical burdens and limit fraud and corruption.

Problems of Monitoring Large Programmes

Many important programmes such as health and family planning are based on an 'outreach' rather than a 'clinic' approach. Large armies of fieldworkers are employed by the government to educate and provide health services to an equally large number of rural clients. In India every male/female in the reproductive age group is covered. Clients assigned to one worker may be distributed in several villages, many of which are not easily accessible. The performance of such programmes is poor because of the unwillingness of the programme worker to spend her/his time in the field. Field-level supervision is also weak. Records of individual clients are suspect because these may not be updated through actual contacts with the client. Manual reporting systems which consume nearly 30 per cent of fieldworkers' time (Bhatnagar and Patel 1988) are ineffective because of the inability of the worker to cope with large amounts of data.

Inadequate Resources

Although outlays on many rural development programmes add up to a sizeable sum, the allocated funds always seem inadequate given the enormity of the development tasks. Most of the available funds are earmarked under specific budget categories. In many programmes, staff salaries account for a substantial part of the budget. There is no discretionary budget with the field-level functionary to do things differently from a standard plan developed at the state and central levels.

■ Venturing into Computerization at the Rural Level

The earliest recognition of the potential of computers in rural development in India came through applied research of some academics during 1975–80 (Patel 1979). A general awareness of the utility of computers was created in the bureaucracy through seminars and training programmes (Computer Society of India 1981). This was followed by a few pioneering experiments in the use of computers by district administrators. By 1988, about 15 districts in India had started using personal computers (PCs) (Bhatnagar 1987; Patel 1986). Some districts were using microcomputers to produce IRDP monthly reports. An interesting application in the health sector was developed at a primary health centre training school located in a *taluka*. In this project a PC was used to store data of couples in the reproductive age in the *taluka*. The system demonstrated how monitoring a programme could be more effective once access to detailed data was available. The system also allowed supervisors to develop detailed activity plans for workers, outlining which couples should be targeted in a given period (Bhatnagar and Patel 1998). A few districts used a PC for monitoring stocks in their public distribution system. At least one NGO (CAM Centre Report 1987) installed a PC in its office to map the resources of a district in Rajasthan. Workshops and seminars were conducted around these experiences (Sanwal 1986). Most of these meetings cited potential benefits but implementation difficulties were ignored.

Most early adopters of IT were district administrators from the elite Indian Administrative Service (IAS). Many IAS officers were young (around 30 years old) and could act independently. However, there were hardly any applications in other important departments such as agriculture, health, or public works, where the district-level heads are older (45–50 years) and are used to executing orders received from their directorates at the state level.

■ Government of India Programme for District-level Computerization

During the period 1978–85, when most of the work discussed earlier was done, a major problem in spreading the use of computers was the need for significant investment in hardware and software. By 1986–87, prices of computers had begun to decline and the availability of locally produced computers had improved. Left to their own momentum, perhaps 50–100 districts would have initiated computerization during 1985–90. When Rajiv Gandhi came to power in 1985, the Government of India decided to increase the pace of IT use at the district level. The National Informatics Centre (NIC)—a central government department—was chosen to implement a national programme called District Information System of National Informatics Centre (DISNIC) to computerize all district offices for which free hardware and software was offered to states (Planning Commission 1989). NIC quickly built up its manpower capability to 2,000 technical staff to undertake the challenge. By 1990, each district computer was connected to a state computer through a local dish antenna and a satellite communication network. The state computer in turn was connected to a computer in New Delhi. This network is called NICNET. The approximate expenditure on the hardware was roughly US$1.5 billion (Rs 6,451.4 crores approx.). Software application development was done centrally for about 15 standardized applications for each district. It was expected that in these applications databases would be created at the district level from which data could be retrieved for central planning. Memorandums of understanding were signed by NIC with each state government, under which state-level cells manned by NIC staff provided support to district-level computerization. NIC was also expected to provide two computer professionals to each district to implement the software.

In a separate programme called Computerized Rural Information Systems Project (CRISP), the rural development ministry and NIC collaborated to develop software for planning and monitoring of IRDP (Ministry of Agriculture 1987). A PC/AT was provided to each District

Rural Development Agency (DRDA) to run the software. State governments were asked to purchase equipment and provide training for their district-level officials. Subsequently, the implementation of the DRDA computerization was also handed over to NIC.

What is noteworthy is that the approach taken by NIC for its district computerization programme was completely centralized. The conception of the idea, spelling out of objectives and choice of applications were all done by NIC. The focus was on developing databases, modelling techniques for planning at the district level and providing relevant information for central planning. The information needs were assessed by a group located in New Delhi and have been treated as standard for all the districts in India. The software design and specification of databases were also standardized and originated in New Delhi. The initial recruitment of personnel and their placement in districts was also centrally done. During the last four years, state-level centres have been set up to provide implementation support to district NIC functionaries. In the CRISP programme, there were a few elements of decentralization. Purchases of hardware and training of district-level functionaries were left to state initiative. No personnel was provided to district DRDAs. However, the design of the software, which included the assessment of required information specifying the type of databases, and the reporting system was centralized.

■ Impact of DISNIC and CRISP on Rural Development Programmes

Commissioning nearly 500 computer centres and a countrywide network connecting these computers was a major achievement. Considering that some district headquarters are significantly away from large cities where most computer vendors are located, maintenance and support of the equipment is reported to be satisfactory. There have been no formal attempts to evaluate the DISNIC and CRISP programmes, but analysis (Bhatnagar 1991; Madon 1992) indicates that computer utilization has been effective in a limited number of districts. On the basis of fieldwork done in 1989–90, Madon reports that the 'manual system still prevails in all the 19 districts of Gujarat and the CRISP system is grossly under-utilized'. In most districts computerization is proceeding at a slower pace than was anticipated. In several districts the DRDA computers are not being used at all. Surprisingly, decision support software supplied by DISNIC and CRISP are not being much used but several local applications have been developed in many districts suggesting that the objectives and priorities of CRISP and DISNIC were not in tune with perceived needs of local administrators. Overall, the impact of this modest expenditure in computerization has been marginal.

The impact of CRISP and DISNIC on administration has been marginal, because the task of changing the administrative culture is enormous. Although IT can be a tool for decentralized planning, integration across departments and reduction in workload, it cannot be the sole instrument of change. Unless district administrators are motivated or held accountable to improve performance of rural development programmes, they will not try a new tool. In CRISP and DISNIC, the effort required to push administrative reforms through the use of IT was grossly underestimated. In a few of the early experiments, computerization in districts did create the intended impact because of the motivation of innovators. However, one could not expect that a similar motivation would exist amongst all district administrators. Very clear pointers from later attempts, such as that in Surendranagar, Gujarat, were ignored. Other organizations which could have shared the tasks were kept away. Finally, the focus of the decision support systems did not quite fit with the past experience of computerization in the state public sector where the primary focus of computerization was on data processing.

In recent years, several state governments have become active in promoting the use of IT. Setting up of the national IT taskforce by the central government has given a new momentum to the development of IT infrastructure and its use in the government sector. In the past, computers were confined to large towns such as district headquarters. Now, at the turn of the century, the growth of telephony, access to VSAT communication and availability of trained personnel in smaller towns, makes it feasible for the government to install computers in small towns and rural areas. The emergence of Internet and web technologies has also given rise to a new paradigm of computing.

■ Types of ICT Applications

ICT applications can be broadly categorized into the following types:

- Decision support to public administrators;
- improving services to citizens; and

- empowering citizens to access information and knowledge.

Each of these types of applications may have different objectives, require different types of technologies to build and, therefore, have different sets of critical success factors.

Decision support systems for public administrators focus on improving planning and monitoring development programmes. Examples of such systems include the use of GIS to plan the location of rural facilities or to identify disaster prone areas. Similarly, provision of PCs in the district rural development agencies was primarily intended to improve the monitoring of the integrated rural developmental programme. The case study of health workers in this volume illustrates how ICT could enable fieldworkers to better plan their activities and for their supervisors to more effectively monitor their performance. Such systems are likely to be successful if the request to build them originate from public administrators interested in improving the administration of development programmes. However, if such tools are provided in a centrally sponsored scheme to administrators unwilling to change their style of administration, that is, who are unwilling to use information and its analysis for decision making, it is unlikely the decision support system will be used. When development programmes are not operationally dependent on such systems, their use becomes purely discretionary.

The second type of applications focus on automating the process of delivering services to citizens, and, in the process, bring in transparency. Examples of such systems are the use of ICT for collecting a variety of payments that citizens need to make to government agencies. The use of ICT can shorten queues and waiting time at collection counters, improve accuracy in billing and accounts receivable and provide immediate proof of payments to citizens. The case study of collecting stamp duty for registration of property deeds, included in this volume, exemplifies the kind of benefits that can accrue to citizens as well as the department delivering the service. Computerization of land records which has been undertaken in many districts is another example. Similarly, issuance of important documents to citizens can also be done through computerized systems.

The last type of applications is concerned with empowering citizens through access to information and knowledge. Access to information about markets is crucial for rural producers of all varieties of goods and services because these must be exported to other regions. Often middlemen, who bring consumers and producers together, are able to seek disproportionate rent because they have access to ruling prices in different markets.

Use of ICT can provide up-to-date information on markets to producers, thus increasing their bargaining power. In spite of a plethora of developmental programmes, citizens are often unaware of free and priced services that institutions are expected to offer them. They are also not aware of the expenditure that different agencies are expected to incur in their village/region and therefore have no way of auditing the performance of development departments. Recently, in a backward region, illiterate villagers demanded information from senior government functionaries in the district regarding allocation of resources for local schemes. They agitated to receive photocopies of such allocations and forced the administration to share this information with the public. ICT can be used to deliver such information through kiosks located in rural areas, some experiments of which are described in this book.

Rural communities can also be helped through access to knowledge that will improve productivity in their work, health practices, and enable them to learn about their environment. A large number of innovations in farm practices, tool design and use of indigenous medication do not diffuse beyond local boundaries because of the isolation of rural communities. Much indigenous knowledge passed down from generations is also becoming extinct due to lack of presentation efforts. ICT and web technologies could make such information/knowledge visible to large cross-sections of rural communities. An organized effort at diffusing such knowledge through ICT—the Honey Bee Network—is described in this volume.

Training programmes to build skills that are in short supply can generate rural employment opportunities. Basic training in ICT can provide employment in electronic repair centres and information handling services. ICT can also be used to train fieldworkers located in rural areas through innovative designs of distance learning programmes. ICT needs to be further deployed to train physically and socially disadvantaged groups.

■ Key Issues in Planning and Implementing ICT Applications

Project Justification

Some IT applications implemented in the past were meant to provide decision support without a clear identification of their benefits in terms of efficiency of the decision making process or better quality of decisions. Several of the successful ICT applications included in this volume were implemented after pilot studies had clearly indicated benefits to all the stakeholders. Even though it may not be possible to specify monetary benefits, it helps to be able to quantify benefits. In selecting applications, costs, benefits and risks have to be balanced. Risks may arise from the quantum of change involved, use of new technologies which have not had extended field use, complexity of the application software, and resistance to the application from vested interests. Often times, simple indigenous technology may be the most appropriate, but there is a tendency to ride the technology bandwagon. Most state governments do not have adequate funds to build ICT applications. They need to raise resources by involving the private sector and/or develop project proposals that are bankable. This requires a clear assessment of costs, benefits and risks. Applications that touch the lives of a large number of citizens are more likely to be able to find benefits outweighing costs.

Multiple Service Centres

There are a number of areas where citizens must interface with government departments to make payments and receive services. Careful analysis must be done to identify the number of citizens that would be benefited by developing ICT applications, because they are expensive and the services need to be located as close to the customer as possible. It is therefore important to select centres that handle multiple services so that benefits accrue to a larger section of the society. Otherwise the benefits may not seen to be commensurate with the costs and investments, particularly in a country like India where there is a perpetual resource crunch and several possible alternative use of funds. Government offices that collect revenues can increase collection provided the process is made convenient. Often community centres (STD booths, TV viewing centres and computer centres for neighbouring schools) can reduce capital investment costs. If such centres serve multiple functions the gap between revenues and costs can be reduced. Convenient access to such facilities is important but it must be remembered that in most of rural India the population has to walk miles even to obtain drinking water. The key issues in designing these systems are the generation of content that would be useful for rural citizens and the trade-off between cost versus convenience in providing access to this content. The content would have to be built in local languages. Tools are now becoming available to view content in Indian languages.

Involve Stakeholders

In the past, national programmes such as DISNIC and CRISP were formulated without adequate consultation with key stakeholders. The key stakeholders were: district-level clerical workers (who entered data and generated reports); heads of user departments (users of the output of the system); state-level departments coordinating computing services; and the NIC staff at district, state and central levels. For the 440 districts about 5,000 officers were affected by computerization. Less than a small fraction of these stakeholders were involved in the process of conceptualizing the programme and defining the scope of different applications.

Now state-level agencies are driving the analysis, design and roll out of new ICT applications. This allows greater involvement of field unit personnel. However, the expediency of rushing implementation may still inhibit a participatory design process. A centralized 'technology push' approach offers the possibility of quick execution but in the end effectiveness could be compromised. A largely technical orientation of executing agency staff can be a handicap in project implementation that requires predominantly managerial skills. Some central agencies executing similar projects have recruited 'hybrids' and managers to successfully oversee the implementation of such projects (El Sherif 1990).

Organizational Mechanisms and Adequate Project Management

It is important to proceed slowly in computerizing at the field level. The most difficult proposition in large-scale computerization is the scaling up from successful pilot sites at a few field sites to a large number of sites spread over a wide geographic area. In the case of DISNIC, during scaling up, the objectives were enhanced further to include networking of all districts. This converted the focus of the project from what should have been a managerial task of diffusing computer applications at the districts to a predominantly technological task of building an inexpensive computer network.

Most of the ICT applications being implemented now present the same dilemma. Wide area networking and communication infrastructure needs to be built before decision support systems or improvement in services to citizens can be implemented. Various organizational models are being tried out to manage these tasks. In Andhra Pradesh the two tasks are performed by separate organizations with a state-level coordination mechanism.

Often the effort involved in managing a large project that is to be rolled out to several field units is underestimated. The skills available to manage such projects are in short supply. A variety of competencies have to be built in the teams handling implementation. These include technology assessment, administrative process redesign, systems analysis and design, project management and management of change. Frequent transfers of senior officers in government also disrupt the execution of large projects.

Sustained Training

Information technology cannot be forced down the throats of unwilling administrators. These public officers need to be motivated to improve the effectiveness of rural development programmes. Once they are so motivated, they will find the technology to be an invaluable tool. IT can support the planning and monitoring effort by making detailed analysis possible. It can create an openness in the administrative system by providing stakeholders access to information. However, administrators need to be convinced about such benefits through first-hand experience, demonstrations and training. Since the purpose of field-level computerization is to improve management, it requires sustained training efforts and technical inputs. Training needs to be oriented towards use of information by workers, supervisors and managers for strengthening, planning and monitoring activities. Field-level officers generally lack training in the use of information. In fact, most field-level managers are seldom trained in management/administration. They have usually had technical jobs before becoming middle-level supervisors.

■ Conclusions

Increasing the effectiveness of rural development programmes is a complex task. The administration has to be energized to face up to the challenge and implement development programmes with honesty and vigour. The rural poor need to be educated and organized to make demands on the administrative system. In all these areas, information technology can play only a supportive role. As regards design and implementation of applications, field officials must get a sense of involvement and ownership.

In discussing the likely impact of ICT on development, a caveat is in order. Some significant successes in transformation of rural communities have had nothing to do with ICT. For instance, a movement called

Swadhyay has enlisted urban professional volunteers to give one or two days of their time to work amongst rural people (Sheth 1992). The movement focused on slow change through repeated contact with rural population focusing on self-help and awakening. Volunteers reach out to rural people asking them to join the movement. Participants have to follow a few basic practices that are essentially focused on self-help, cooperation amongst communities and contribution of a part of one's time to communities. It is not possible to sketch this in detail but literature is now available on recording the transformation of whole communities through this movement over a period of five to 10 years. Men have been weaned away from alcoholism. Cleanliness has been brought in villages and productivity increases in agriculture has resulted. A significant increase in the level of well-being has been felt in the basic transformation attitude that it is indeed possible to transform one's life.

Clearly improved literacy, particularly of females, can have a lasting impact on rural poverty. However, another kind of education which focuses on self-help, understanding one's own political rights, and more open access to information can lead to transparencies in resource allocation and reduced corruption. This kind of education does not necessarily come from the traditional schooling system. It cannot be provided by an inefficient and corrupt bureaucracy. (NGO movement such as *Swadhyay* can play a significant role.) A major stumbling block is the poor quality of governance and lack of participation by the poor in governance. The only way this can be improved is through a greater sharing of information and better communication amongst the concerned stakeholders.

References

Avgerou, C., 1990, Computer Based Information Systems and Modernisation of Public Administration in Developing Countries, in, Bhatnagar & Bjorn Anderson (ed.), *Information Technology in Developing Countries*, North Holland.

Bhatnagar, Subhash, 1987, Decision Support for District Administration: An Experiment in Surendranagar, *Informational Technology for Development*, in, P. Sadanandan (ed.) Tata McGraw-Hill, New Delhi, pp. 43–52.

———, 1991, Impacting Rural Development through IT : Need to Move Beyond Technology, in, M.L. Goyal, (ed.), *Information Technology in Every Day Life*, Tata McGraw-Hill, New Delhi.

Bhatnagar, S.C. and Patel, N.R., 1988, Decentralized Computing for Rural Development, *OMEGA*, 16(2), pp. 165–70.

CAM Centre Report, 1987, National Workshop on Computers in District Administration, IIM Ahmedabad, February 9–11.

Computer Society of India, 1981, Informatics 81, An International Symposium on Informatics for Development, CSI, February.

El Sherif, H., 1990, Managing Institutionalization of Strategic Decision Support for the Egyptian Cabinet. *Interfaces* 20(1), pp. 97–114.

Government of India, 1984, Planning Commission, Report of the Working Group on District Planning, vol. I, May, New Delhi.

————, 1989, Planning Commission, District Information System of National Informatics Centre, New Delhi.

Hooja, R. and **Mathur, P.C.**, 1991, *District and Decentralized Plannings*, Rawat Publications, Jaipur.

Madon, S., 1992, The Computerized Rural Information Systems Project, in, Subhash Bhatnagar (ed.) Manpower and Training Needs, *Information Technology Manpower: Key Issues for DCs*. Tata McGraw Hill, New Delhi, pp.171–79.

Ministry of Agriculture, 1987, Computerisation of Rural Development Information, Department of Rural Development, Ministry of Agriculture, New Delhi.

Patel, N.R., 1979, Locating Rural Social Service Centres in India, *Management Science*, 25(1), pp. 22–30.

————, 1986, Computers and Rural Development in India. Paper presented at APDAC, Kualalumpur.

Paterson, A., 1982, *Development Planning Lessons and Experience*, John Hopkins University Press, Baltimore.

Roy, B., 1991, Rural Uplift: Grass without Roots, *Times of India*, February 23.

Sanwal, M., 1986, *Computer Applications in District Administration,* Administrative Training Institute, Nainital.

Sheth, N.R., 1992, Children of the Same God. Working Paper, Gujarat Institute of Development Research.

PART II

Decision Support to Public Administrators for Improving Planning and Monitoring of Developmental Programmes

2

Electronic Support for Rural Healthcare Workers

NARESH KUMAR REDDY AND MIKE GRAVES

The India Healthcare Project began in 1994 as a collaborative project between the Government of India, Apple Computer, Inc., and CMC Ltd, India. The project's initial impetus came from the Indian government's interest in providing electronic support to village workers in their rural healthcare system. The healthcare workers were burdened with demanding data collection and paperwork responsibilities, which affected the quality of their work and their ability to provide primary healthcare services to the people they serve. The project team designed a system based on the Newton handheld computing technology, with the intent of lessening the paperwork burden, improve data accuracy and empower the village healthcare worker to provide timely care and information. The project has reached the end of an investigation and research phase and has been turned over to CMC Ltd for further development.

■ Introduction

In the fall of 1994, the India Healthcare Project began as a collaborative effort between the Government of India (GoI) and Apple Computer. As the project began to unfold, other partners from India's information technology and design industries became central to the project. Its purpose was to provide research and initial testing of an electronically based support system for rural healthcare in India.

India's healthcare system includes a very large rural system administered by the GoI. The system is hierarchical, starting from the health minister and percolating down to community healthcare workers, who go on house-to-house visits in rural areas. According to the 1991 Census, the system provides healthcare for a rural population of 630 million people in 32 states (GoI 1995).

Initial collaboration between the GoI and Apple Computer spelt a possibility of providing portable laptop computers to healthcare workers in the villages. These workers, Auxiliary Nurse Midwives (ANMs), are the system's direct point of contact with the people. By design, each ANM is responsible for administering to 5,000 persons, typically distributed over several villages and hamlets. She (ANMs are exclusively women) operates from a sub-centre, located in or near one of the villages under her charge. The sub-centre includes her office, with registers and other items needed for paperwork, dispensary materials, first-aid materials and other medical supplies. Often the villages and hamlets she serves may be located many miles apart. She calls on the houses within her charge once every month. She is not provided with any transportation facility by the government. Her duty is to collect basic demographic data, administer immunization, advise on family welfare and educate people on mother–child health programmes. Figure 2.1 shows an ANM with villagers under her purview.

In its meetings with Apple Computer, GoI representatives were introduced to the Newton Message Pad, a new product introduced by Apple in 1993. The Message Pad provided advantages exceeding those of laptop computers. It was lower in cost, worked much longer on its internal batteries, was smaller in size and lighter in weight and, therefore, even more portable. It also provided for pen-input and interaction, thus requiring less keyboard and mouse skills. The health ministry was intrigued with the Message Pad's capabilities and decided to use it for a research project aimed at supporting the work of the village healthcare system.

In accordance with the GoI's aim to support its fieldworkers, a team from Apple Computer adopted a grassroots strategy and began observing

Figure 2.1 An ANM at work

and learning about the work of the ANMs in the field. A study site was selected in cooperation with the government, in the state of Rajasthan, near the city of Ajmer. The location was chosen as one that would be representative of other sites throughout the country. It possessed a moderately equipped technology infrastructure for the introduction of the new technology and practices. It offered a good chance to learn what the requirements and chances of success would be for introducing similar technologies in other parts of the country.

A number of factors made it imperative that Apple's team form collaborations with Indian companies to carry out the research phase of the project and to provide a vehicle for ongoing development after the research phase was completed. The Apple team was a research group whose charter did not extend beyond prototyping and field study phases of the project. To engineer and maintain a new system of technology support would require a permanent presence and availability. In addition, in order to gather knowledge of the ANMs' work practices and functions, local knowledge, transportation, access to healthcare personnel and facilities and a general local presence would be needed. The two partners Apple chose to work with were the Centre for Diffusion of Information Technology (CDIT) and CMC Ltd, headquartered in Delhi, with offices throughout India. The CDIT in particular could provide coordination and communication to the government along with knowledge of the field site and the healthcare structure. CMC is an established technology development leader within India, capable of providing an ongoing development team, field maintenance and a research and development centre in Hyderabad.

As the project unfolded, the National Institute for Design (NID) in Ahmedabad also became indispensable. A student from NID served as an intern on the project and provided continuous field presence that Apple's team could not maintain.

■ Objectives of the Project

To provide support tools that would allow ANMs to reduce time spent doing paperwork: ANMs fill in a battery of periodic reports and deliver them to their supervisors, who in turn deliver data to a 'computor' who generates summary analyses to proceed up the system's reporting chain. This data gathering function provides factual information on the rural population's growth, birth rate and immunization rate. Filling out the periodic reports by hand is laborious and time-consuming. The Newton-based electronic system would enable automated report generation on the basis of the daily entry of data during or after the ANM's rounds.

To increase the accuracy of the data supplied by the ANMs through the healthcare reporting structure: The paper-based data system requires redundant data entry (i.e., various forms requiring the same baseline data along with special reports) with no provision for consistency. Moreover, the reported data may be inconsistent or incomplete. The electronic system would minimize or eliminate redundant data entry, perform consistency checks as well as provide checks for allowable data values and provide a permanent storage system for archiving the needed data.

To provide a means for getting healthcare data at the village level into an electronic form: The computor's job, in the paper-based system, requires producing a number of summaries, all composed by hand. Electronic data submission and compilation would not only ease the current process but would also make more ad hoc, focused data analysis possible.

To provide the ANM with information that helps her to provide more effective service to the villages within her responsibility: In the paper-based system, ANMs get little or no feedback from their data submissions. They do not get time-based summaries, trend-spotting, or data-derived alerts. The Newton device would provide the basis for an on-demand information system for her to consult, so as to enable her to reflect on current conditions within her villages via the device. This information would include not only data summaries but also downloaded educational materials relevant to conditions as they develop.

■ Investigation

The first three site visits, from the fall of 1994 to the spring of 1995, were devoted to learning about various aspects of the healthcare system, the ANM's job, and the various challenges faced. The following are the principal goals of the visits:

- Learning about the physical environment of the field site: The area around Ajmer is a desert with typical sub-centres that lack indoor electricity or telephones. It was required to know about the existence of technology in rural areas in the form of fax machines, village telephones and postal systems.

- Learning about the official healthcare hierarchy, reporting system, and data flow: To achieve this, paper models of the reporting structure and data flow were constructed. These were later cross-checked with CDIT's understanding and with persons at different levels within the structure itself.
- Learning how the ANM does her job: This involved not only knowing her official functions as set out under the healthcare system, but also her informal practices and roles within the village. Her job was reconstructed from the standpoint of her concerns and priorities. To do so, a 'card study' method was developed and employed, enabling the ANMs to reconstruct their practices and priorities.
- Learning to learn more: This included locating and contacting the key persons, sources of information and also people who would offer support to the project.

■ Technology Used

The major part of the project was investigative. Before any technology could be designed or implemented, it was desirable to know the significant details, the design of the healthcare system and the work practices and concerns of the ANMs.

Accordingly, technology choices, other than those already mentioned (choice of the Newton Message Pad as a platform), were put on hold until field investigations were undertaken and an understanding of the ANM's job and its context within the healthcare system could be spelt out. The methodology was 'user centred' in the sense that technological features of the system were to be designed on the basis of this understanding. Subsequent design stages included the direct participation of ANMs to provide feedback, test hypotheses, offer suggestions and speculate on its uses.

The platform for design was the Newton Message Pad. The Newton technology (Newton Toolkit), now no longer in production at Apple, provided an operating system and development environment amenable to fast prototyping and modification. While the Message Pad product distributed in the United States and Europe featured handwriting recognition as a primary means of data input, it was not feasible to provide similar features for the Indian system. The ANMs in the field site would not be able to use it, as only a few could speak, read or write English. Hindi was the common language. Providing Hindi recognition would have been a very formidable project in itself; it was thus decided to have an on-screen keyboard for data input.

It was desirable to provide the ANMs with a system that was in tune with their practices, priorities and conceptualization of their work. The first task was to ensure an appropriate data structure that would also provide a basis for navigational organization.

The hierarchy from sub-centre to couples mirrors data structures currently represented in the ANM's existing paper registers. The most critical design task was that of the system's user interface. The system designed would later be termed an 'electronic register'.

After numerous paper designs and mockups, an interface was developed. Its basic design was readily acceptable to the ANMs. Some important features of this design are as follows:

Navigation based on iconic representations of villages, households, families, couples and individuals.

Figure 2.2 shows the reconstruction of an ANM's work practices. Figures 2.3 and 2.4 show the main navigational screen and the data backbone respectively. Figure 2.5 shows the view of a household containing two families.

Figure 2.2 Reconstructing the ANM's work practices

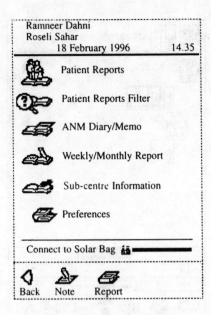

Figure 2.3 Main Navigational Screen

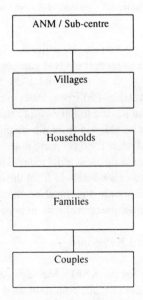

Figure 2.4 Data Backbone

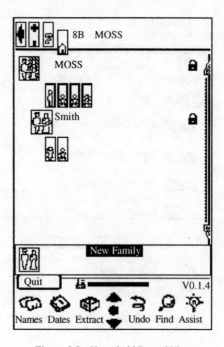

Figure 2.5   Household Record View

Moss is the head of a household, while the Smith family shares the house with them. At a glance, the ANM can see that the Smith family includes two children, i.e., an infant and a pre-adolescent. Each icon, when tapped by the Message Pad's pen, leads to more specific record of that individual. Without having to tap down to the individual record, the individual's status can be gleaned from the state of his icon. Immunization status, disease and other conditions are noted by shadings, markings and other modifications to the individual icons. The ANM gets an overall impression of the status of a household from the representation. She can add data, such as enrolment in a prenatal healthcare programme and the icons will change to show the appropriate new status.

Customized Font and Keyboard

The design of the font for the ANM's Message Pad required tailoring to meet the needs of the hot climatic conditions and non-backlit display of the Message Pad 120. In addition, Alexander Grünsteidl, the principal interface designer of the project, supplied a range of fonts and styles for various interface elements (buttons, field labels, menu items, etc.). The keyboard itself is based on the Indian Script Code for Information Interchange (ISCII) standard, with modifications to allow the normally invisible, shifted keyset to remain visible in the background of the unshifted keyset (ISCIE 1991). Hindi does not include a distinction between upper and lower case characters, but it does contain too many characters to be included in a single keyset (see Figure 2.6).

Modifiable Text Constants

Since a prototype for a system was provided to be used in many parts of India, it was important to design a means for changing easily the on-screen text, script and language. In fact, the prototype includes the capability of switching back and forth between English and Hindi on-screen texts and, in principle, any other required language. Text constants and

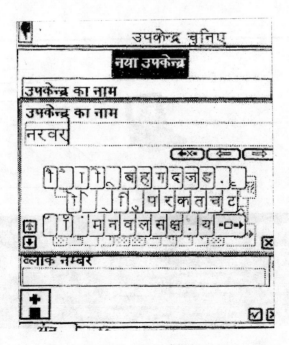

Figure 2.6 Customized Keyboard

font selections are kept separately from the main software code and can be altered without significant engineering skills. This feature became especially important because of the variation not only of language, but also of dialects within languages that differ from region to region.

■ Overall System Design

The system design (Figure 2.7) provides for linking ANMs' Newton's clients with a desktop machine, held at the supervisor's level. The supervisor's desktop machine will receive compiled reports from the ANMs, back up their software and data, and provide educational materials in electronic form as downloads to the ANM's Message Pads. Selection of downloaded material is based on the requirements of the ANM's reports. Thus, for example, when new cases of malaria show a rise beyond a set threshold, prevention and treatment materials can be automatically supplied in electronic form viewable by the ANMs on their Message Pads.

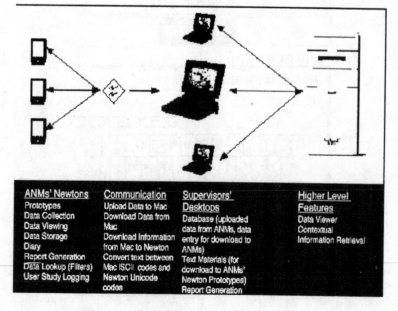

ANMs' Newtons	Communication	Supervisors' Desktops	Higher Level Features
Prototypes	Upload Data to Mac	Database (uploaded	Data Viewer
Data Collection	Download Data from	data from ANMs, data	Contextual
Data Viewing	Mac	entry for download to	Information Retrieval
Data Storage	Download Information	ANMs)	
Diary	from Mac to Newton	Text Materials (for	
Report Generation	Convert text between	download to ANMs'	
Data Lookup (Filters)	Mac ISCII codes and	Newton Prototypes)	
User Study Logging	Newton Unicode	Report Generation	
	codes		

Figure 2.7 System Overview

■ Implementation Challenges

The pilot project faced cultural, geographical and social as well as technical challenges..

Cultural and geographical challenges: The Newton technology was relatively new and its development environment unfamiliar, but even more challenging were the unfamiliar cultures, languages and geography of India. The engineering teams from CMC as well as from Apple were not well oriented with the rural area of Ajmer. Besides eating, boarding and lodging, communication with ANMs and others within the healthcare system required translators. These translators, however, quickly grew to occupy expanded roles not only as interpreters of what was worded, but also what was intended and felt.

Subtle challenges in international collaboration had to be faced. Work between geographically separated teams (Apple in Cupertino, California, and CMC in Hyderabad, India) carries its own difficulties, including dealing with time differences, differing communication styles and infrastructures. Moreover, participation in the project has different degrees of importance and meanings to an Indian engineer and to one working in California. The two companies, Apple and CMC, also have different priorities, interests and expectations from the project. All need to be balanced so as not to unintentionally sabotage well-meaning efforts.

Social challenges: The Indian healthcare system is vast and ambitious. Apparently no one seemed to comprehend the system completely. Introduction of this technological support system would have social effects. In the most informed of situations, armed with a theory of social interactions in the system into which we were introducing our innovation, social impacts would still be unpredictable. A major challenge then was to maintain respect for existing relationships of authority and responsibility, while introducing an innovation that would produce changes.

One major area of change would be the future roles of the ANM, supervisor and computor. Currently, the paper-reporting system circumscribes a large part of their work. However, now that data is electronically entered, stored, submitted, compiled and analyzed, how would their jobs change? Would the computor be able to transfer his data-analysis role to a computing environment? How would the availability of ad hoc reports and analysis change his role in the system? Would the ANM be able to devote more time to interaction with villagers? Would she be able to cut down the time spent on preparing reports? If so, would her priorities change? How would the supervisor's relationship with the ANM change, as he would be able to see compiled reports with consistent data uploaded to a desktop? Would this reduce his role, or would it empower him to spend more time in training and coaching?

The second question concerned the future position of the ANM within the village. The ANM often comes from an area other than the villages she serves. She is often better educated than the villagers. After equipping her with an expensive electronic device, a handheld computer, would the perceived distance between her and the village community increase? How would the handheld device alter her conversations with villagers during her rounds? Knowing that computers are more distinctive and less common in India than in western environments, care was taken not to refer to the device as a computer and to avoid encouraging the ANMs to carry the device with them on their rounds.

Technical challenges: In addition to challenges posed by the multiplicity of languages and scripts, and the team's lack of familiarity with the new Newton technology and handheld interfaces, a number of technical challenges cropped up from the physical environment and rural infrastructure.

Figure 2.8 The Paper-Reporting System

The Newton Message Pad can be equipped with a rechargeable battery pack. However, its battery life is not sufficient to rely on the sporadic availability of electricity in the ANMs' everyday environment. Batteries are expensive and cumbersome to carry and change as required. With the cooperation of Keep It Simple Systems, the team designed and tested a customized carrying bag for the Message Pad, incorporating a solar panel to continuously charge the Message Pad within the bag. The bag itself was modelled after bags commonly carried by the ANMs to hold registers, immunization supplies and other items. The solar bag also provides some measure of protection from rains.

Dust is a major problem in the desert environment of rural India. The Message Pad's serial port and the screen itself are particularly vulnerable to dust and sand. It is, as a standard, equipped with a rubber cover for the serial port and a lid to cover the display screen when not in use. Despite this, dust could pose a problem. We experimented with a stretch-to-fit rubber boot for the device, which would also cushion against accidental bumps and drops. In addition, we tried out a clear plastic protective cover for the display screen, which could remain in place during use. These challenges may get magnified as the application of this system gradually increases. Awareness at this initial phase might help in smoothening out some of the practical problems that are at present anticipated.

■ Implementation Results and Benefits

The India Healthcare Project has reached the end of its preliminary phases. It is too early to report results on a definitive, large-scale nature. Rather, our current results are qualitative and are drawn from controlled field exposure (Graves et al. 1998). The purpose of these field exposures has been to provide input for iterative design of the support system.

However, the first results were impressionistic and very positive. ANMs showed no hesitation in using the device, taking the pen in hand and tapping on the screen. Some had experience with keyboards and took easily to using the software version. Some even reported using the keyboard as 'fun'. They saw the parallels between the electronic system and their paper registers, coining the term 'electronic register'.

Overall, although quantitative results are still unavailable, the ANMs believed that the system would be helpful to them. They saw that redundancies in data entry would be eliminated or at least reduced. The prospect of automated report generation made a very favourable impression.

They felt that an initial training period, perhaps of one month duration involving one-to-one coaching, would be sufficient to make the device an integral part of their job.

The device's display of the ongoing design was too dim and glare from the sun too great. Later tests with a new, backlit display are expected to show considerable improvement. Much of the on-screen text produced difficulty. We had in many cases simply translated English text, such as 'open' or 'cancel', into Hindi equivalents. Such translations were very sensitive to local dialect and language subtleties that even our native Hindi-speaking translators could not foresee. This led to our placing a greater emphasis on a simple technical procedure for modifying and localizing on-screen text.

The actual practices of the ANMs were very different from the official accounts of their procedures and responsibilities. Many of the techniques of data collection capability included in our prototype could not be used. Others were inaccurate with respect to actual practice. Consequently, a further effort undertaken with increased leadership from CMC, focused on a reduced, simplified prototype.

■ Conclusions

Based on the pilot study, we draw the following conclusions.

- To provide support tools that would allow ANMs to reduce time spent in paperwork: The Newton-based electronic system would help in expediting work. This would not only save hours of tedious labour but also leave her with ample time and energy to devote to the people she serves.
- To increase the accuracy of data flowing up from the ANMs through the healthcare reporting structure: Although quantitative measures are required, the initial results seem to be promising. Elimination of redundancy and consistency checking would reduce the ANM's paperwork. It is yet to be discovered how entering data into the electronic device will actually fit into her daily routine. Maximum time would be saved if she carried the device with her on her rounds and entered the data directly. However, not all ANMs do this even with the paper register system. They often take notes in a diary, which are later transferred to registers in their sub-centre office.

The automated report will not only save time and effort for the ANM but also for the supervisor and computor by eliminating laborious hand compilation and calculation.

- To provide a means for getting healthcare data at the village level into electronic form: This goal is well served by the existing prototype. The questions that will now need to be answered include how the solutions will scale over other regions of India and what effects the electronic medium will have on roles and relationships within the reporting structure and on significant changes it may make possible for ad hoc analysis, generation of timely information and empowerment of the ANMs for more directed healthcare activities.
- To provide the ANM with information that allows her to provide more effective service to the villages within her responsibility: Drawing conclusions with respect to this goal would be premature at this stage as the system has not yet been fully implemented.

The team from Apple Computer has completed its participation in the India Healthcare Project. Further pilot studies and larger scale implementation is in the hands of CMC Ltd. Given the discontinuation of Newton technology, other handheld computing platforms will need to be examined. However, the results of the field investigation and prototype design are likely to achieve desired results.

References

Government of India, 1995, Bulletin on Rural Health Statistics in India for the Quarter ending June 1995, Rural Health Division, Ministry of Health and Family Welfare, Nirman Bhawan, New Delhi.

Graves, Mike, Grisedale, Sally, Grünsteidl, Alexander et al., 1998, Unfamiliar Ground: Designing Technology to Support Rural Healthcare Workers in India. SIGCHI Bulletin, Association for Computing Machinery, New York.

Indian Script Code for Information Exchange—ISCIE, 1991, Bureau of Indian Standards, New Delhi.

3

Technological Challenges of the Disaster Management Plan for the State of Maharashtra

KRISHNA S. VATSA

Maharashtra has become the first state in the country to implement a comprehensive disaster management plan (DMP), complete with a state-of-the-art satellite-linked computer network connecting various civic bodies, collectorates and blocks in the state. The project was conceived after a massive earthquake devastated the districts of Latur and Osmanabad in September 1993. This paper describes the information network established under the project providing a coordinated response strategy for the state.

■ Introduction

The disaster management plan for the state of Maharashtra represents one of the most innovative and significant examples of what an imaginative and reform-oriented public administration can accomplish to minimize the effects of any natural disaster. It showed how synergy, shared goals and vision among different stakeholders produced outstanding results in a limited timeframe.

The project started against the grim and tragic backdrop of the earthquake of 30 September 1993, which killed around 8,000 people in the districts of Latur and Osmanabad, injured 16,000 and destroyed 53 villages. The damage to the living environment was colossal and irreparable. The state government received assistance from the World Bank, which signed a Memorandum of Understanding (MoU) with the Government of India (GoI) within a week of the disaster, to support the rehabilitation efforts. The Maharashtra Emergency Earthquake Rehabilitation Project (MEERP) was drawn up with a planned outlay of $300 million (Rs 1,290.3 crores approx.) and implemented over a period of four-and-half years. It is one of the country's largest rehabilitation programmes in terms of households and area covered. Nearly 250,000 families took part in the reconstruction programme.

Though the GoI signed the development credit agreement with the World Bank, no concrete steps were taken until one year after the MEERP commenced. The first workshop, which was attended by officials and experts, was organized in May 1995; almost a year after the World Bank loan became effective. The project authorities were totally preoccupied with the spadework required for this massive rehabilitation programme. There was a lull again for a year till mid-1996 as the project went through a very critical phase, with a number of destabilizing developments.

However, the MEERP acquired a steady course in mid-1996, and the disaster management plan as an activity picked up. The Government of Maharashtra (GoM) appointed national and international consultants to assist in the preparation of this plan, with the support of the UK Department for International Development (DFID). At the same time, the United Nations Development Programme (UNDP) showed interest in strengthening MEERP. The initial goal was to develop the state plan and pilot plans for six districts. The UNDP support made it possible to cover all the remaining districts of the state. This support also coincided with the GoI's decision to assist the state government in setting up a centre for disaster management. The GoM located the centre in Yashwantrao Chavan Academy of Development Administration (YASHADA), Pune, and the apex training organization of the state government. It was envisaged that this centre would grow in the process of preparing the disaster management plans for the remaining 25 districts. The UNDP support was made available for institution-building in YASHADA, as well as for the preparation of district disaster management plans. The synchronized support of the World Bank, DFID, UNDP, GoI and GoM to the disaster management plan helped in achieving its far-reaching agenda.

The disaster management plan presented a risk-assessment and vulnerability analysis, explained the command and coordination structure, set up the operating standards, created a resource directory and laid down a mitigation strategy. These plans are area-specific and have been prepared on the basis of an impressive database created for all the districts. The World Bank organized a review meeting of the DMP in Washington in June 1997, which was attended by Bank officials, DFID and UNDP experts and GoM officials. The three days of a full-scale presentation of all the plan documents by the GoM proved to be a watershed event for the DMP.

The GoM's presentation received complete approval and support of all the multilateral agencies. The World Bank immediately agreed to extend support for the setting-up of control rooms, communication network and the Geographical Information System (GIS)-based DMP for the entire state. The DFID decided to renew its support to this activity through a fresh grant. The DMP thus emerged from the shadow of the MEERP to become a full-fledged programme. It entered the implementation phase. It was the beginning of a challenge as all these activities had to be completed in a period of 18 months, the period of credit left for the MEERP. The work plan for all activities is highlighted in Table 3.1.

■ Implementation Activities

The need for critical support to the disaster management functions of the district administration has been felt for a long time. However, there was an inadequate articulation of the support required. There was an occasional demand for a wireless network connecting the collector (the bureaucrat in charge of the district) to the sub-divisions and *talukas*. It did not, however, lead to an organized move within the government to augment

Table 3.1 Work plan of activities

Activities	Budget		Start date	End date
Phase I (World Bank-supported)	(in million US $)*	(in Rs million)		
VHF communication network	2.3	99	Feb 98	June 99
VSAT communication network	3.1	136	May 98	July 99
Setting up emergency operation centre in *Mantralaya*	0.2	7	Apr 98	June 99
Setting up district control rooms in all the districts	0.9	40	Oct 98	June 99
Creation of GIS-based disaster management information system	0.8	36	Dec 97	June 99
Setting up e-mail network (GoM-supported)	0.7	34	Feb 99	July 99
Phase II (DFID-supported)				
Creation of GIS-based disaster management information system	1.7	74	Oct 99	Sep 02
Training & simulation programme	1.0	45	Oct 99	Sep 02
Community vulnerability reduction programmes	1.0	45	Oct 99	Sep 02
Total	11.7	516		

* At the conversion rate of 1 US$ = Rs 43.01 (June 1999).

the communication facilities. However, the planning for disaster management brought up prominently the operational requirements of the planned activities. The need for setting up well-equipped control rooms was felt unanimously by all concerned. The communication network was an essential facility required for operational support. While the government officials were familiar with the support the Very High Frequency (VHF) network would provide, the Very Small Aperture Terminal (VSAT) network came up as a new initiative. To provide connectivity between districts, divisions and state headquarters, independent of the department of telecommunications (DoT) lines, the VSAT network was a recommended alternative solution. When the World Bank agreed to support all the implementation activities proposed by the GoM after the review meeting in Washington, it was decided to commission the VSAT network.

The VHF and VSAT network was expected to provide a very dependable communication network even in case of heavy rains when the terrestrial line is the first casualty and long-distance connectivity is lost. In a disaster situation, the combined efforts of communication lines with the district authorities and line departments form the key to organizing response operations. Thus, building these represented the first priority of the government.

The GIS-based disaster management information system (DMIS) evolved out of the planning activities for disaster management. The collectors of the state were of the view that planning evacuation and exit routes in case of natural or chemical disasters was much simpler if the GIS support was available. The GIS would also help them locate their resources much better for deployment in disaster-affected areas. The Maharashtra Remote Sensing Applications Centre (MRSAC), Nagpur, had done some work in developing GIS-based applications. The maps were prepared for different kinds of hazards for all the districts. The hazard maps, on a 1:250,000 scale, show all hazard-prone settlements and identify disaster management infrastructure facilities such as government offices, hospitals, police and fire brigade stations. The maps also show road and rail networks and the river system. These maps could give the collectors an accurate idea of the area and population affected by a natural calamity or an accident, as also how resources could be sent to those affected.

The DMIS would also be helpful in all kinds of planning and development efforts. With the combined efforts of the DMIS and UNDP, the maps were started on 1:250,000 scale. And once the World Bank gave its support, they were done on a 1:50,000 scale for all districts except Mumbai.

This became a detailed exercise for mapping of resources as well as socio-economic attributes.

Though these facilities have not been fully commissioned, the officials have started using them. In a number of districts, the collectors used the wireless network during the floods in 1998. Similarly, a number of departments are using the GIS database for a range of functions.

■ Intra-district VHF Communication Network

The decision to set up a semi-duplex VHF network for intra-district communication was taken after assessing all the other options in terms of cost and reliability. The VHF communication network would provide a reliable and cheap means of communication, independent of terrestrial lines, between the districts, sub-divisions and *talukas*. It would provide a civil wireless system to the civilian administrators throughout the state at a cost of approximately $2.4 million (Rs 10.32 crores approx.). The GoM commissioned a topographical survey of the entire state in the course of preparing the feasibility study for the VHF network. As part of this network, a total of 600 base stations, 56 repeater stations, 190 mobile stations and 150 handheld sets were installed. At present, the network has become fully operational in 11 districts. The construction and electrification of repeater stations, located at remote and inaccessible sites, took considerable time. The completion of repeater rooms will make the entire network fully operational throughout the state. The VHF networt is working smoothly in those districts where it has been commissioned. It is planned to train regular staff to operate the wireless sets, without creating any additional posts. The GoM would maintain the network through an annual maintenance contract after the end of the warranty period.

■ Inter-district VSAT Network

To provide a fail-safe means of non-terrestrial communication, the GoM took a decision to set up the VSAT network, connecting the state headquarters with the divisional and district headquarters. In the course of preparing the feasibility survey, it was decided to set up a closed user group, with two hubs and 37 control rooms. The main hub would be in *Mantralaya* in Mumbai, with a stand-by hub in YASHADA, Pune. The communication network (Single Channel Per Carrier–Demand

Assigned Multiple Access, SCPC–DAMA) is capable of providing a variety of telecom services including voice, data, facsimile and video-conferencing. There is exclusive transponder space for the VSAT network, which means that the GoM will not utilize the satellite resources on a shared basis with other users. The process of linking the Pune district headquarters with all the 37 control rooms has been completed.

When the GoM was planning for the VSAT network, the INSAT–2D failed. With the approval of the DoT, the GoM approached the Videsh Sanchar Nigam Ltd (VSNL) and secured the transponder space in INTELSAT. It is a KU band network and the GoM is one of the first in the country to use it. The process of commissioning the VSAT network has been beset with commercial and shipping problems, as it is a highly import-intensive network.

■ Implementation Arrangements for VHF and VSAT Network

The GoM appointed the procurement, engineering and system integration consultants for the installation and commissioning of both communications networks. The consulting firm selected was Maharashtra Electronics Corporation Ltd (MELTRON), a state public sector undertaking, on a sole-source basis. Considering that the implementing organization would fold up after the completion of the MEERP, support from a government organization like MELTRON to maintain the networks was considered essential.

The consultants prepared the bid documents, organized the pre-bid conference and evaluated the bids for final recommendation. Incidentally, both the bids of the VHF and VSAT were awarded to the same contractor. This could have given the contractor the advantage of scale of operations. However, poor commercial support and inadequate managerial strength dogged the process of implementation.

■ E-mail Network

The GoM decided to utilize VSAT connectivity in all the districts of the state to provide a closed user group intranet e-mail to all the government offices. To install e-mail network, the GoM decided to procure and install high-end server class computers, routers, modems and hubs in *Mantralaya,* YASHADA, and in all the offices of the commissioners and collectors.

The GoM is organizing the necessary software support, which would also enable the staff to correspond in Marathi (the regional language of the people of Maharashtra). Though the procurement of e-mail network is an extension of the VSAT network, which is reimbursable by the World Bank, its cost will be borne by the GoM.

The GoM has assigned the procurement contract to the same contractor who is installing the VSAT network. The contractor would procure the hardware and peripherals and integrate them with the software being supplied by the GoM. It was realized that the extension in the scope of VSAT procurement to cover e-mail would cut short the time required for a fresh bid consideration and achieve synchronization. The capacity of e-mail network was sized, and the specifications for servers, routers and modems fixed after extensive consultations with the technical experts. The entire architecture of the network was proof-checked to verify its optimal functioning.

■ GIS-based Disaster Management Information System (DMIS)

The GoM assigned the work of creating the DMIS to MRSAC, a GoM organization specializing in remote sensing applications. The MRSAC was chosen for several reasons. First, the digitization of the spatial data would require a great deal of interpretation of the satellite imagery, which constituted the strength of MRSAC. Second, the MRSAC also has the necessary equipment and expertise in GIS. Third, the entire database of districts needs to be updated periodically, which only a government organization like MRSAC could do on a regular basis non-commercially. Finally, the need to protect confidentiality of such a large database weighed in favour of selecting MRSAC, also on a sole-source basis.

MRSAC was also appointed the procurement consultant for computer hardware and software for all the districts. The GoM procured computers for all the commissioners and collectors, along with the GIS software of Arcinfo and Arcview. The procurement has been organized so that all software upgrades available in the next five years would be made available to all offices in the state. MRSAC has organized a training programme at the state and divisional levels.

In creating the DMIS, the following steps were taken:
- Creation of base maps;

- procurement of satellite data;
- interpretation of satellite data;
- collection and compilation of non-spatial data;
- computerization of spatial and non-spatial data;
- integrated analysis of spatial and non-spatial data and generation of hazard maps;
- transfer of digital database to district authorities;
- development of shell query and updating of facilities;
- training of district officials and assistance in implementation.

The DMIS on a 1:250,000 scale for all the districts has been completed. The digitization of data on 1:50,000 scale has been completed for 17 districts in the first phase of activity, supported by the World Bank. In the next phase, supported by the DFID, digitization of remaining districts will be completed. The elaborate query design too will be taken up in the next phase.

MRSAC secured the remote sensing data from the National Remote Sensing Applications Centre, and got it interpreted through a number of sub-contractors in the private sector. Once the thematic maps were made available, they were checked by experts and were validated with ground-level findings. After the validation, the digitization of these maps would be done at MRSAC, and the physical and socio-economic data attributed to the maps. The important inputs in this exercise are the remote sensing maps and physical and socio-economic data. Further, it requires intensive work to digitize this data.

Though the primary objective of the DMIS is to plan for disaster management, the database has been organized in such a way that it could be extensively utilized for resource planning. A number of departments, such as water supply, water conservation, public works and forests, are using the database for their own applications. The MRSAC has decided to appoint one GIS specialist for every division, and one for *Mantralaya*, to provide hardware and software support to all the officers for developing and using GIS applications.

■ Control Rooms

To physically locate the communication network and GIS-based DMIS, it has been decided to set up control rooms in *Mantralaya*, divisional commissioners and collectors' offices. The GoM has developed a standard layout for all the control rooms, and is organizing architectural support throughout the state to set it up. In most of the districts, a control room equipped with all the facilities has now been set up.

■ Facilitation

The GoM seized the opportunity offered by MEERP for a very ambitious exercise in capability building in the area of disaster management. Handling all these activities simultaneously, in addition to the main responsibility of rehabilitating the earthquake-affected, was extremely demanding of Project Management Unit (PMU) officials. The biggest challenge was coordination with all 31 districts in implementation of these activities. It was a combination of determination to accomplish these objectives and professional standards we set for ourselves that saw us through the entire project.

There were a few significant organizational advantages. First, there was the Central Implementation Group (CIG), headed by the chief secretary, which took all policy decisions in respect of the MEERP. But the work was extremely simplified once the CIG approved all the implementation activities in a single meeting. The support of the highest echelons of the GoM was crucial for these activities. For instance, the installation of e-mail network was an afterthought, and thus required a great deal of spadework to fit into the original procurement of the VSAT network. However, support was available for this activity at the highest level in the government.

Second, the World Bank was very supportive of the disaster management plan and related activities. The World Bank's involvement ensured that procurement decisions were taken with concern for quality, due attention to economy and transparency of process.

Third, all the procurement decisions were taken within the PMU. The PMU was technically competent to address all the issues of procurement and to take decisions without reference to the planning and finance departments for these decisions.

Fourth, the PMU was a small set-up, headed by the secretary, and supported by a deputy secretary, financial advisor and chief engineer. It was a small cohesive group, which could think and act collectively.

■ Sustainability

In terms of design of the system, all the components are to be used in normal functioning. None of these activities is meant exclusively for a disaster situation. It would ensure that all the facilities are used extensively and maintained by the concerned authorities. The VHF, VSAT and e-mail networks are normal communication lines, which are to be used by all responsible state functionaries. Their normal time functioning would provide sustainability to these systems. The GoM has also decided to provide a regular budget for these activities so that aspects of maintenance are well taken care of.

Once the warranty period is over, the VHF and VSAT networks will be maintained by annual maintenance contracts. As part of the maintenance contract for the VSAT, the hub in *Mantralaya* will be manned 24 hours a day. Eight communication engineers will be appointed to run the Emergency Operations Centre (EOC) on a round-the-clock basis in three shifts in Mumbai. If the hub in *Mantralaya* goes down, the stand-by hub at YASHADA, Pune, will be activated. In the six divisional commissioners' offices, there will be one engineer to attend to maintenance requirements of the division.

For the e-mail network, one communication engineer per shift (two shifts per day, six days a week) will be located at the Mumbai hub. In each of the divisional commissioners' offices, one additional engineer specifically for e-mail will provide maintenance support. To maintain the GIS-based DMIS, there will be three GIS specialists, one in state headquarters and two in Aurangabad and Pune.

The GoM will not create posts of engineers for the VSAT and e-mail networks since it believes these specialities should be outsourced to the private sector. Similarly, MRSAC will recruit the GIS experts on a contract basis.

The PMU, which was in charge of implementing the MEERP including all the disaster management activities, will be merged with the department of relief and rehabilitation upon the completion of project activities on 1 June 2000. This department will maintain the control rooms, communication networks, GIS database and annual maintenance contracts through its annual budget.

■ Service Levels

In the contract for two communication networks, service levels have been specified. The uptime performance for the VSAT network is 99.5 per cent. There are penal provisions in the contract if this level of performance is not maintained. The service level for the VHF is 95 per cent. The service level for the e-mail network has not been specified, as it is contingent upon VSAT connectivity. A plan book is being developed for the use of GIS. It would contain all possible queries on disaster management and other applications and types of databases available at the district level.

■ Key Implementation Issues

Certain important issues emerged through the implementation of these activities. First, the importance of elaborate groundwork must be under-scored. Before the proposals were presented to the government and the World Bank, a feasibility study was undertaken on the proposed commu-nication network. The study also showed what the GIS was capable of achieving. Both the network and the GIS were presented as an organized effort in capability building of the state government. Had these activities been taken up individually, the impact and visibility would not have been the same.

Second, there must be an organized effort within the government to appreciate the need for these critical facilities and implement them. If the government as a collective body is not committed to the implementation of these activities, there is little chance of such initiatives reaching their fruition. Wherever there was less supervision and control over these ac-tivities by the divisional commissioners, the work suffered.

Third, the certainty of financial allocation for this activity, which was made available through the World Bank, has been a great confidence building factor. Fourth, the World Bank procurement procedures for the engagement of consultants and contractors have been clearly defined and relatively easy to follow, unlike those of the state government which are lengthy and tedious, and where there is scope for political interference.

Fifth, a government set-up comprising administrators, procurement experts, engineers and financial managers is more suited to take up these activities, with its diverse requirements, as compared to a regular depart-ment with a conventional staff structure. When the GoM decided to take up e-mail network on the strength of VSAT connectivity, it was done through an innovative procurement procedure. It was done as an exten-sion of the World Bank-supported VSAT network, though the GoM has supported the cost of installation and commissioning. These procedural innovations were possible because of the professional capacity of the PMU.

Finally, the level of commitment to accomplish the stated mission is extremely important. Through the course of the rehabilitation programme, the Earthquake Rehabilitation Cell cultivated an image of efficiency and professionalism. To sustain this image, it was important that the entire department show a great deal of commitment to accomplish these tasks in a fixed timeframe.

■ Constraints

There were noteworthy constraints in executing all the activities within a well-defined timeframe. It was a very difficult task to attend to all the details of implementation, spread over the entire state. Besides, coordinating with six divisional commissioners and 31 collectors all over the state for a number of activities required a great deal of time, effort and tenacity. It was one of the biggest administrative challenges for us. Some of the specific problems we faced in respect of individual components are as follows:

Contractor management: The biggest problem we faced was the inability of the contractor to abide by the implementation schedule. An activity that we planned to complete in 100 days was performed in almost 400 days.

Geographical remoteness: The second problem was setting up of repeater stations in remote sites. Some of the sites suggested were under forestland, and situating a repeater site on this land became a serious problem for us. Some of the other repeater sites were to be located on hilltops, and constructing the room and electrifying it took a lot of time. It took us almost a year to complete these 56 repeater stations all over the state.

VSAT network: The VSAT network ran into all kinds of procurement problems. The contractors could not obtain the import licence in time. Further, they could not open the Letter of Credit for a long time, and this delayed the whole activity considerably. There were shipping problems, delaying the delivery of antennas. The commercial management of the project left a lot to be desired. The constraints in setting up the VSAT network emanated from the inexperience of private sector subcontractors in handling import-intensive assignments, such as the VSAT network. A competing supplier, who obtained a contract for a separate VSAT network for the Maharashtra police, tried, unsuccessfully, to put forth the police network for use by all state administrators.

Control rooms: Though three rounds of architect's meetings across the state were organized for setting up control rooms in all the divisional and district headquarters, the whole exercise of constructing and equipping the control rooms took about nine months. The collectors were advised to set up control rooms by employing an architect from the market, in the government, but as there is a strong tendency to rely on the public works department in the construction efforts, the setting up of this facility was delayed.

GIS-based DMIS: MRSAC delivered the entire output in the assigned time. However, the database that was to be compiled by the district administration and sent to the MRSAC took considerable time. As a result, the socio-economic attributes have not yet been ported on the database.

■ Conclusion

All these activities for disaster response, when fully completed will provide a new paradigm in connectivity and database availability in the state. The capability of all state agencies in terms of dealing with information flow and decision making will be significantly enhanced. However, preparedness and quick response of various agencies to minimize the effects of any natural disaster and to utilize the computer and communication equipment also requires continuous training and orientation of the officials at different levels. In the final analysis, the toughest challenge lies in changing the attitude and mindset of state functionaries to implement the DMP and guarantee that relief operations begin within the shortest time possible once any disaster strikes.

PART III

Improving Services to Citizens and Bringing in Transparency

4

IT at Milk Collection Centres in Cooperative Dairies: The National Dairy Development Board Experience

RUPAK CHAKRAVARTY

In recent years, the cooperative movement initiated by the National Dairy Development Board (NDDB) has led to a substantial increase in milk production in India. The two main reasons for this increase are the efficient collection of milk and higher profit for the producers, both of which have, to some degree, been influenced by IT. The appropriate information technology described in this paper helped to make information symmetric in the market, thereby minimizing problems of adverse selection and corruption.

■ Introduction

The farmer-owned Amul Cooperative in Anand, Gujarat, has become a model for all dairy development projects in India. This model showed that an integrated approach along cooperative lines could enhance production, procurement, processing and marketing of milk. Based on this success story of the 1960s, the Government of India launched Operation Flood nationwide in 1970. This project was modelled on the Anand Pattern Cooperative and established organizations similar to Amul in other states of India. The purpose was to provide a regularized and standardized link between the rural milk supply centres and the urban demand centres.

The core of the project is the village milk cooperative. According to the Anand Pattern, a village cooperative society of primary producers is formed under the guidance of a supervisor or milk supply officer of the Cooperative Dairy Union (district-level cooperative owning the processing plant). A milk producer becomes a member by paying a nominal entrance fee. He must then agree to sell milk only to the society. The members elect a managing committee headed by a chairman. This committee is responsible for the recruitment of staff who is in charge of the day-to-day operations of the society. Each society has a milk collection centre to which the farmers take their milk in the morning and evening.

Starting with 18 milk sheds or collection centres in the first phase, Operation Flood now organizes marketing of milk from 179 milk sheds in over 500 towns. These milk sheds form the catchment area from where milk is brought into the cities. In addition to organizing milk collection and marketing, the cooperative also standardizes methods of procurement, processing and quality control of milk, assuring the producer/farmer of fairness in these procedures. The number of farmers organized into village milk producers' cooperative societies is now 1,000,000 and the daily procurement of milk by the cooperatives is 13,000,000 litres.

Milk is procured from the farmers at the village cooperative societies and is then sent to the district cooperative dairy union by trucks in cans or by tankers from the bulk coolers located at the villages. It is weighed and tested for fat at the dairy docks and is then pasturized. The dairy then converts the milk into liquid milk for sale and various milk products as per the product mix provided by the state-level dairy federation, which markets the products of all the dairies in the state. Surplus milk from the dairies, after meeting the local liquid milk requirement and converting into various products, is then sent to the Mother Dairies situated in metro cities by road or rail milk tankers (40,000 litre capacity). Liquid milk is generally sold in urban centres in plastic pouches, which is packed at the district dairies. In metros, milk is also sold through bulk vending booths, where consumers can obtain a measured quantity of milk by inserting a coin in an automatic machine.

A National Milk Grid has been formed by linking deficit areas with the surplus areas, thus assuring proper marketing of milk and hence an assured return to the rural producers. For example, milk is sent across a distance of 2,200 km (1,375 miles) from Anand in Gujarat to Calcutta in West Bengal by rail tankers.

■ Problems in the Conventional System

1. Quality control was a major problem that confronted the cooperatives. The NDDB worked to reduce quality variations among sellers by upgrading the technology of milk production by improving cattle feed and milk processing and delivery infrastructure.
2. Fair and efficient markets do not occur by accident, they are created.

Thus, the cooperatives had difficulties to ensure accuracy in measuring quantity and fat content of milk and in making fair payments to the farmers.

3. Before automation, the farmer was paid only every 10 days. Therefore, even though at times he/she delivered milk each day, the farmer was not sure of the reliability of manual calculations of quality and quantity by cooperative society staff.

4. Milk for testing was stored in plastic bottles and tested only after the milk collection process was over. This led to unhygienic conditions and fear of contamination at the centre.

5. The conventional Gerber method for testing the fat content of milk is a cumbersome multi-step method. It has various disadvantages including chances of human error, handling of corrosive chemicals and use of different types of glassware. All these processes added to the cost and the time taken to test the milk.

■ Technology Used

The importance of speed of operations should be emphasized, because 600 milk collection centres receive milk from 60,000 farmers daily. On an average, if the saving in terms of time per farmer were 10 minutes every day, it would amount to a huge saving to the tune of 10,000 hours per day! The deployment of technology was considered instrumental to realize such savings.

Electronic Milko-Tester

The conventional Gerber method takes about two or three hours to ascertain the fat content of milk. This in turn delays the payment to the farmer as he is paid strictly on the quality of milk. To overcome this, a milko-tester was developed by a Danish firm which was later modified to milko-tester minor, a less complicated version of the milko-tester III. This model is not only economical but also simple to operate. Moreover, it is suited to village conditions. The greatest advantage of this tester is the accuracy coupled with the rapidity of analysis of fat content. It works on the principle of light scattering with manual homogenization. It operates on AC-mains as well as on battery, with a built-in battery charger and an automatic switch-over to the battery in case of power failure. Rajasthan Electronics and Instrumentation Ltd (REIL), in collaboration with M/sA/SN Foss

Electric, Denmark, started the commercial production of milko-testers in 1981 and sold about 26,000 units to dairy cooperatives all over India.

The Micro-processor Based Milk Collection System

Milko-testers reduce the time taken to ascertain the quality and the fat content of milk, which in turn helps in overcoming all associated problems of the traditional method of testing such as storage of samples and handling of corrosive chemicals. However, the calculation and payment of bills remained as cumbersome as ever since they were still being calculated manually. The NDDB, in 1988, took up a project to develop an integrated milk collection system to effect immediate calculation and payment of bills to the farmer. For this REIL and M/s ATE Enterprises Ltd developed prototypes that were tested in two villages in Kheda district, namely Mogri and Bedwa.

REIL Developed Milk Collection System: (see Annexure for technical specifications). This system has been operational in Mogri for the past several years. It consists of three pieces of equipment, as shown in Figure 4.1, placed alongside each other: (*a*) Electronic Milk Tester (EMT); (*b*) Milk Weighing System (MWS); and (*c*) Data Processor (DP). The printer is a supplementary piece of equipment.

The EMT and the MWS are interfaced with the Data Processor (DP). This system needs only three operators. Under this system, each farmer is given a plastic card with a code number as his/her identification. The DP reads the identification on the card and the farmer pours his milk into a steel trough over a weigh-bridge. The weight of the milk gets displayed to the farmer and instantaneously gets transferred to the DP in litres. The first operator fills the cans after the milk has been weighed, while the second takes a 5ml sample of the milk and holds it up to a tube of a fat testing machine. The hand lever of the machine is then moved thrice and the fat content of the milk sample is displayed on the monitor and also transferred to the DP. A small printer attached to the DP gives a slip that reads the farmer's name, quantity of milk, percentage of fat and the amount of payment to be made. The calculations of the payment are made on the basis of a rate chart, as the price of the milk depends on its fat content. With this slip, the farmer can collect his/her money from an adjoining window. The payment is rounded to the closest rupee value and the balance is credited to his account the next day. The entire process takes about 20 seconds. The DP has the added advantage of storing the transaction of milk collection of all farmers of the shift. At the end of the shift the machine prints out the individual transactions along with the grand totals.

Other functions made possible by this system are:

- Entry of year, date, cow/buffalo milk fat rate, shift and membership number into the DP at initialization;
- erasing and rectifying any incorrect data that may have been fed in inadvertently;
- independent displays of weight and fat content by the MWS and the EMT on individual display ports;
- storage of weight and fat content figures in the memory of the DP and immediate printout of all necessary details to each farmer;
- a memory capacity to hold data for up to 1,000 farmers; and
- data can be sent online to a PC via RS232C serial communication at the end of a shift.

Figure 4.1 Micro-Processor Based Milk Collection System

ATE Enterprises Ltd Developed Milk Collection System: This system has been operational in the Bedwa district for the past several years. The system is similar to the one developed by REIL except for some additional functions such as:

- A digital display port facing the farmer showing the farmer's code number, quantity of milk, the fat percentage and the total amount of money to be paid to the farmer;
- a battery backed RAM for the DP to enable storage of all transactions for a period of 11 days. After this the DP can be attached to a standard dot matrix printer which prints out all the transactions. This ledger is then sorted and processed by a ROM-based programme.

PC-based Milk Collection System: The micro-processor based milk collection system facilitates speedy collection of milk, an efficient and accurate measurement of fat content and quick payment to the farmer. The PC-based system not only enhances the speed of services at each cooperative, but also increases the efficiency and reliability of overall operations. Among other things, it:

- stores individual milk collection details on a suitable storage device for yearly analysis;
- facilitates the complete financial accounting of the cooperative society;
- maintains records of cattle feed, ghee[1] and other local milk sale of the society;
- monitors animal breeding, health and nutrition programmes; and
- maintains records of members, for instance, details of their land-holdings and animals.

The benefit of IT to the societies is manifold. The number of people required for the manual procedure has come down. Daily accounts can be obtained immediately. The computer can, within moments, calculate the profits of the society on the basis of data received from the dairy, regarding the payment made to the milk society for the previous day's collection. The income and expenditure incurred by the society can also be incorporated. Perhaps most significantly, the farmers are now ensured of correct and honest payments.

■ Implementation Problems

The project to develop a PC-based integrated system that the NDDB took up in early 1991 was initiated in Ranu, a village in Baroda district. This system, however, did not function for long because of particular problems. First, the PC/XT failed as it could not withstand the excessive dust and extreme climatic conditions. Besides, the weighing system failed frequently.

However, with improvements in technology the PCs have become more rugged and can now be operated in village conditions. This underlines an important aspect of IT applications that needs attention, i.e., our heavy reliance on imported technology. The desire to develop a region-specific technology has now been felt.

■ Technological and Financial Support

When the NDDB financed the project in early 1990s for the micro-processor based Automatic Milk Collection Station (AMCS), the cost was about $2,250 (Rs 96,800 approx.), which included the micro-processor, weighing machine, milko-tester, an 80 column dot-matrix printer and a UPS. Prices have now come down and the entire set is available for about $1,800 (Rs 77,400 approx.).

In terms of technological support, intensive training was given to the operators. Service engineers on motorcycles provided quick maintenance whenever required. Virus-proofing of the systems was also taken care of and back-up procedures for data were defined.

The NDDB has financial support from the untied foreign assistance funds and the government budget in addition to other sources to sustain technological upgradation requirements. The Board has financed 200 such units under a scheme of 30 per cent grant and 70 per cent loan under Operation Flood III, with a view to popularize this system in villages.

■ Private Sector Development

Two Indian entrepreneurs gave considerable impetus to this project. They offered an integrated system to the societies and at times even offered to install the system free of cost until the customer was convinced of the utility and satisfied with the performance of the system.

Many new entrepreneurs have now started manufacturing these instruments with improved features. In the initial stages, cooperative dairy unions also provided loan facilities to village societies for the purchase of the system. REIL has also supplied a large number of AMCS to milk cooperatives in Rajasthan and Punjab. The IT-based systems have now become so popular that village societies are buying systems with their own funds.

However, the uphill task of developing the market was left to a few private enterprises. Only if a large number of private sector enterprises are involved can the application of this technology be adopted all over India.

■ Implementation Benefits of the AMCS

Farmers were the main beneficiaries of this project. Figure 4.2 shows farmers queuing up at the AMCS.

The main benefits of the AMCS as compared to the conventional methods are as follows:

Figure 4.2 Farmers at the AMCS

- Immediate payment for the milk delivered;
- accurate information about fat content, quantity of milk and payment due to the farmer is displayed;
- accuracy in weighing the milk on the MWS as against the manual process where milk was weighed using measuring containers which very often led to a financial loss to farmers;
- immediate testing of the quality of milk as against testing after two to three hours of collection;
- the card reader unit ensures speedy operation and an error-free entry of identification number of the farmer; and
- the elimination of manual registers for all kinds of information and data storage.

■ Conclusion

In Gujarat, 573 AMCS are currently in operation. Kheda has the highest number of AMCS (278), followed by Sabarkantha (74), Surat (68), Mehsana (53), Banaskantha (29), Panchmahal (18), Bharuch and Vadodara (15 each). Gandhinagar, Ahmedabad and Rajkot have 10, 8 and 5 AMCS respectively.

The cheap and credible technology described in this paper illustrates how the delivery system has been improved by ensuring prompt payment to the farmers and instilling their confidence in the cooperative set-up, as also minimizing the problem of adverse selection and defeating corruption. It is one of the several ways in which the NDDB has dealt with problems by using state-of-the-art technology. Other improvements and innovations have been in breeding and feeding technologies and in processing and delivery infrastructure.

Notes

1. Ghee is fat prepared from butter.

Annexure

Equipment Specifications

1. ELECTRONIC MILK TESTER (EMT)

a.	Electronics	:	State-of-the-Art Micro-controller Based Electonics
b.	Measuring Range	:	0–13% Fat
c.	Capacity	:	120–150 Samples/Hr
d.	Accuracy (Sd)	:	0–5% Fat –0.06% 5–8% Fat –0.10% 8–13% Fat –0.20%
e.	Repeatability	:	0–5% Fat –0.03% 5–8% Fat –0.04% 8–13% Fat –0.08%
f.	Sample Volume	:	0.5 ml / Test
g.	Diluent Volume	:	6.5 ml / Test
h.	Calibration	:	One Calibration Channel Adjustable Within the Range 0–13%
i.	Power Supply	:	AC-220/240 V Maximum +10% Minimum –15% DC-12V, Motor Car Battery. A Fully Charged Battery Will Last for at Least 10 Hours Operation
j.	Interface	:	Parallel Digital Port Provided on Rear Panel 9-Pin D-Type Connector for Data Processor
k.	Auto Zero Facility	:	Zero Setting at the Push of a Button. Auto Zero Inhibit Function to Prevent Manipulation of % Fat Display
l.	Ambient Temperature	:	5ºC to 45ºC
m.	Dimensions (LXWXD)	:	23 × 31 × 53 cm

2. MILK WEIGHING SYSTEM (MWS)

a.	Electronics	:	State-of-the Art Micro-Controller Based Electronics
b.	Principle	:	Load Cell Based Operation
c.	Measuring Range	:	0 to 20 kg
d.	Resolution	:	+ 10 gms
e.	Accuracy	:	+ 20 gms
f.	Repeatability	:	+ 1 Digit (+10 gms)
g.	Linearity	:	0.02%
h.	Power	:	230v 50 Hz AC/12 V. DC

i.	Interface	:	Parallel Digital Port Provided on Rear Panel VIA 15-Pin D-Type Connector for Transfer of Data to Data Processor
j.	Container	:	Stainless Steel Container of Capacity 15 kg for Weighing Milk
k.	Operating Temperature	:	+5°C to 50°C Range
l.	Display	:	7-Segment Led Dual Display on Flag Staff
m.	Overload	:	Safe Max Load: 150% of Rated Load. Ultimate Overload: 200% of Rated Load

3. DATA PROCESSOR (DP)

a.	Electronics	:	State-of-the-Art Micro-controller Based Electronics
b.	Inputs/Outputs	:	Two 8-Bit Digital Input Channels, One RS 232C Port for PC Interface
c.	Data Display	:	6-Digit 7-Segmented Display/Dual Display on Flag Staff Optional
d.	Control Inputs	:	Through 4 × 4 Hex Keyboard with Special Keys & Standard Numeric Keys, 0–9
e.	Printer	:	21 Column Dot Matrix Printer
f.	Power	:	230V, 50HZ, AC, +10% / 12 VDC
g.	Memory	:	16 K RAM 16 K EPROM
h.	Battery Back-up	:	3V, Nicad Battery
i.	Ambient Temperature	:	+5°C to 45°C
j.	Dimensions (LXWXH)	:	47 × 30.7 × 17.2 cm

5

Computer-aided Registration of Deeds and Stamp Duties

J. SATYANARAYANA

Land registration offices throughout Andhra Pradesh are now embellished with computerized counters under the Computer-aided Administration of Registration Department (CARD) project. The project is directed at altering the antiquated procedures that have governed the registration system, affecting sales of urban and agricultural properties. Citizens now complete registration formalities within an hour. The CARD project illustrates some of the key implementation issues, state and national governments shall face in their efforts to use IT to improve citizen–government interfaces. The registration system is governed by antiquated procedures, which include the laborious copying and indexing of documents as well as their unscientific space-consuming preservation in ill-maintained backrooms. The laborious procedures and lack of transparency in property valuation resulted in a flourishing business for brokers and middlemen who exploited citizens selling property. The CARD project is an attempt to reform this system through the use of IT.

■ Introduction

Since time immemorial, immovable property has been a key determinant of a person's socio-economic status. Agricultural land is the most significant factor of economic well-being in rural areas. The system of recording and documenting the changes in ownership and transactions involving immovable property is equally ancient and important. The first major attempt in India to consolidate and codify procedures and practices relating to registration of documents resulted in the enactment of the Registration Act in 1908. This Act specifies the process and types of documents that can be registered. The registration process is a systematic though antiquated way of recording a document or deed. It confers a legal status to the document and provides a measure of security to the transaction. As a result, registration of deeds is of vital public importance—both in urban and rural areas.

The system recording of deeds on stamp paper is governed by the Indian Stamp Act of 1899. This Act aims to derive revenues for the state. Deeds of various kinds are required by law to be written on stamp paper of prescribed value, although in some states there is provision for the document to be written on plain paper with a payment of a stamp duty. Deeds are predominantly written on stamp paper. The preference of the public for stamp paper arises out of its aesthetic and authentic look, besides the quality of the paper that can last for over a century. Thus, it is likely to be in demand for a few more generations despite technological changes.

■ Significance of Registration of Deeds

The increasing demand for stamp paper for purposes of writing documents brings with it a host of management issues. Beginning with the management of the manufacturing process of judicial and non-judicial stamp papers of different denominations (Re1 to Rs 25,000) at the government security press, the supply chain from the Central Security Press at Nasik, Maharashtra, to over 500 treasuries spread across the country has to be monitored. Inventory management, security in storage, sales of stamp paper to vendors and end users and management of document writing facilities require vigilant monitoring and control.

The Stamp Act lays down the rates of stamp duties leviable on different types of instruments. The Act specifies some 62 types of instruments, but sale, gift, partition, mortgage, lease, exchange and agreement constitute over 95 per cent of all documents. There are two broad methods of levying stamp duties on different types of instruments: *ad valorem* duty and fixed duty. In the *ad valorem* method, the stamp duty is charged as a percentage of the value of property or loan that is the subject of the instrument. This method ensures an inherent level of buoyancy in stamp revenues and also accounts for over 90 per cent of the total revenue from stamp duty. Fixed stamp duty is levied on miscellaneous instruments such as partnership, chit, agreement, supplementary deed and trust deed. This is primarily to give legal status to the instrument rather than to generate revenue.

Stamp duty confers legal status to instruments. It is also a significant source of revenue to the government. The gross revenue derived from stamp duties in Andhra Pradesh (AP) in 1997–98 was approximately $5,140,714 (Rs 22.11 crores). The significant contribution of stamp revenues to the exchequer leads us to two conclusions:

- Improvements in the administration of the duty through modernization, computerization and taxation reform is likely to yield sizeable monetary results and favourable cost-benefits.
- Creation of a fairly rigid, equitable and transparent system of levy would result in a high degree of satisfaction among the otherwise unwilling and grudging taxpayers.

■ Procedure for Registration of a Document

The conventional 13-step registration procedure is complex and time-consuming, and beyond the comprehension of most citizens. It involves:

Step 1   Ascertaining the value of the property;

Step 2   calculating stamp duty, transfer duty, registration fee and other fees payable on the instrument;

Step 3   purchase of stamp paper;

Step 4   getting the legal document written;

Step 5   procuring the necessary certificates to be enclosed with the document;

Step 6   presentation of the document to the sub-registrar of the jurisdiction;

Step 7   scrutiny of the document by the sub-registrar;

Step 8   valuation of the property by the sub-registrar, calculation of stamp duty, transfer duty, registration fees and miscellaneous fees;

Step 9   payment of deficit stamp duty, if any;

Step 10 admission of execution by the executant before the sub-registrar and two witnesses;

Step 11 copying of document into the register books;

Step 12 posting entries to 2 indexes (by name and property), accounts and reports; and

Step 13 return of the document to the citizen.

To go through this cumbersome procedure, someone selling a small or large plot of land has to go to various government offices and private firms that deliver the various services for the entire registration process. The following is a brief account of the various service agencies involved in the process:

Stamp vendors: Stamps are sold to the public through private stamp vendors licensed by the registration and stamps department and through stamp counters located at the offices of the sub-registrars. The private stamp vendors charge an illegal premium on the face value of the stamps when there is scarcity of stamps of a particular denomination. They also resort to sale of fake stamps and post-dated stamps for an additional charge. There are about 2,300 licensed stamp vendors and 221 departmental stamp counters in AP.

Document writers: The public relies heavily on professional document writers, advocates and solicitors. The document writers have been given official recognition in several states of India through a system of licensing (AP has 3,908 licensed writers). In AP, when a document is not written by a licensed document writer, an additional fee (approximately $5 or Rs 215) is levied at the time of registration. Document writers provide a comprehensive service. They prepare maps and location sketches to describe the property and fill in various forms, besides guiding and assisting citizens in procuring the certificates from various authorities. They charge a fee much higher than that prescribed.

Registration agents: These are self-employed individuals and firms who get a document registered, covering the whole range of services, for a lump sum amount.

Registration offices: The legal procedure of registration takes place at the office of the sub-registrar of assurances. In AP, there are 387 sub-registrar offices that register about 120,000,000 documents a year. The work of the sub-registrar is supervised by district registrars (28), deputy inspectors (6) and the inspector general (1) who form a pyramidal hierarchy.

■ Problems of the Manual Registration System

In order to justify the need to modernize, it is necessary to understand and appreciate the following problems of the conventional manual process of registration.

Age-old procedures and practices: The registration department is highly procedure-bound, conservative and rigid. The complicated procedures are not only time- and energy-consuming but are also not easily comprehensible by citizens. People thus turn to brokers to get their job done.

Lack of transparency in valuation: Since liability of stamp duty is related to value of the property, valuation becomes a vital function. A system of market value guidelines or basic values was introduced in 1975 whereby the rate per unit of rural/urban lands is assessed for all villages/towns and incorporated in a register for public guidance. But, the basic value registers are usually not accessible to the public, and even if they were, it is difficult for a common man to read them and calculate the amount of stamp duty, transfer duty, registration fee and miscellaneous fee. All this creates an impression that the valuation of property is 'flexible' and 'negotiable'. This lack of transparency in valuation thus brings with it a host of corrupt practices.

Tedious back-office functions: Conventional manual methods of copying, indexing and retrieving documents are laborious, time-consuming and prone to errors and manipulations. Thus a premium is usually attached to speedy delivery of services.

Mystification: The laborious procedures and lack of transparency is the cause of the flourishing business of brokers and middlemen who exploit the mystified air shrouding the registration process.

Preservation of documents: The conventional method of copying documents[1] into registers creates problems in preservation. The registers take a lot of physical space usually in ill-maintained backrooms. They also deteriorate qualitatively with age and repeated handling.

■ Genesis of the Idea

The idea of introducing computers originated in 1988 when a project was initiated to computerize the process of issuing Encumbrance Certificates (ECs).[2] A 386 server operating with 14 dumb terminals was set up at a cost of about $31,000 (Rs 13.3 lakhs). Data entry of index registers of the twin cities of Hyderabad and Secunderabad was initiated with technical assistance from the National Informatics Centre (NIC). The entry of 15 years of data went on until 1995 when a pilot scheme for issuing ECs on computers was launched in one of the city offices.

The feasibility of taking up a comprehensive Registration Department computerization project to address other registration formalities and problems was established in a systems study conducted by the author in August 1996. The study brought out methods by which the various registration services could be delivered electronically across the counter in an integrated manner. It spelt out how the process of valuation could be consigned to the computer, besides, it also introduced the concept of electronic document management as an essential part of computerizing the registration process.

Pursuant to the study, a pilot project for computerizing two sub-registrar offices (SROs) was sanctioned at a cost of about $55,000 (Rs 23.7 lakhs). The pilot sites were inaugurated on 8 August 1997 and 9 September 1997. Encouraged by the success of the pilot projects, the Government of Andhra Pradesh sanctioned approximately $360,000 (Rs 1.55 crores) in September 1997 for extending the project to other SROs (212). Thus began an intensive effort to implement the CARD project.

■ Objectives of the CARD Project

CARD (Computer-aided Administration of Registration Department) is a major IT project, designed to eliminate the maladies affecting the system of registration through electronic delivery of all the registration services. It is based on the following primary objectives:

- Demystify the registration process;
- introduce a transparent system of valuation of properties easily accessible to citizens;
- bring in speed, efficiency, consistency and reliability;
- replace the manual system of copying and filing of documents with a sophisticated document management system that uses imaging technology;
- replace the manual system of indexing, accounting and reporting;
- introduce electronic document writing; and
- substantially improve the citizen interface.

Besides the primary objectives, this project aims to fulfil the following secondary objectives:

- To cater to different levels of users;
- to provide for adequate security levels;
- to deliver all the registration services across the counter;
- to bring in maximum user-friendliness;
- to be scalable;
- to permit modular development and implementation;
- to enable migration to a network computing environment in the future; and
- to be easily adaptable to statutory changes in registration procedures.

■ Architecture of the CARD System

The CARD system has three layers of master data and one layer of transaction data.

The CARD master data: This layer contains the master data that is created at the state level and is common throughout the state. It can be modified only by the specific authority of the commissioner and inspector general of registration at the state level. CARD masters include registration office codes, village and habitation codes, rates of stamp duty, transfer duty and registration fee, standard unit rates for valuation of structures, depreciation rates, codes for different classes of instruments and codes for different classes of lands. The users at the district and sub-district levels can only read/print this master data but not alter it. This safeguards the system from possible alterations detrimental to the state's revenue. Such a control also enhances the credibility of the system among the public.

The SRO masters: This layer contains the master data relevant and applicable to the jurisdiction of an SRO. It can be altered only under the authority of the district registrar. It contains the basic values (rates per acre/sq. yard) of all the land within the SRO, survey-number-wise and house-number-wise for agricultural and residential/commercial properties and a list of villages falling within the jurisdiction of the SRO.

The SRO user: This layer contains data relating to the transactions handled across the counter in the SRO. It is the user-level data entered by the operators on a transaction basis. Most of this data cannot be altered by the operator. This prevents unauthorized alterations/interpolations to the valuable registration data, which affects the rights and liabilities of citizens.

The CARD system handles a wide variety of transactions. These include registration of deeds, cash transactions, market value assistance, issuing ECs and delivery of certified copies. It scans the documents registered and 'cuts' the images into a CD-ROM for preservation and archiving. It also keeps a record of inventory of different denominations of stamps, sale of stamps and accounts relating to all monetary transactions.

■ Technology Used

The CARD software has been designed and developed using a client–server architecture. The server stores and processes all the master and transaction data. The clients contain the business logic and form the front-end at the counters to handle various transactions.

■ The 'ABC' Approach

Since volume of the registration transactions varies widely among the SROs, an 'ABC' approach was adopted to optimally match the hardware and software configurations to the requirement of different sized SROs. Accordingly, the SROs have been divided into A, B and C categories based on the number of documents registered and the revenue derived from each office as shown:

Category	No. of offices	No. of documents registered (per year)	Revenue (per year) (Rs in millions)
A	41	Above 5,000	Above 500
B	95	2,500–5,000	250–500
C	78	1,500–2,500	75–250

The configuration of the various items of hardware and software packages is indicated in the Annexure. By optimizing the configuration of hardware systems, a maximum number of offices could be covered within the constraints posed by the budget.

■ Design of Service Levels and Delivery Channels

Service levels: The CARD project aims at improving the quality of services offered by the registration department by providing a computer interface between citizens and government. The service levels are now substantially enhanced. The tedious procedures that took weeks are now accomplished in just a few minutes. Market value assistance and issuing of the EC will take five minutes each. The sale of stamp papers, document writing and registration of the documents will take 10 minutes, 30 minutes and one hour respectively.

The positive impact of the CARD project on the efficiency of registration operations can be gauged from Table 5.1.

■ Design of Forms and Reports

A set of bilingual (English and Telugu) forms and reports have been designed and printed in the required number of copies. The forms include:

Table 5.1 Quantitative benefits

Description of registration service	Time taken in manual system	Time taken in CARD system
Valuation of properties	1 hour	10 minutes
Sale of stamp paper	30 minutes	10 minutes
Document writing	Not available	30 minutes
Registration	1 to 7 days	1 hour
Encumbrance Certificate	1 to 5 days	10 minutes
Certified copies of documents (registration under CARD)	1 to 3 days	10 minutes

- Requisition form for market value assistance;
- input form to accompany the document to be registered (urban property);
- input form to accompany the document to be registered (rural property);
- indent for purchase of stamp papers; and
- application for issue of an EC.

Reports (pre-printed stationery) include:
- Market value report (check slip);
- registration check slip;
- EC; and
- cash receipt.

The reports/check slips to be handed over to the citizens have been printed in different colours with the logo of the project and the emblem of the government for an attractive and authentic look.

CARD software: The CARD system has been designed by the author. The application software has been developed by the NIC and Fortune Informatics Ltd. After development of the application software which runs the CARD system, each feature was thoroughly discussed, demonstrated, refined, tested and modified. Close links and coordination between the field officers and the development team made it possible to modify the software to make the system deliver all the services to the expected level of efficiency. About 15 man-years of effort have gone into the development of this system. Eight versions of the software have so far been released for implementation across the state within a span of about four months. The focus of development has now shifted from 'functionality' to security.

■ Implementation Challenges

Implementation of an IT project in a government department across the state involving over 200 locations is a formidable challenge, especially, because of the rapid technological advances in this field. The project needed to be finalized and implemented rapidly, so that the technology, both hardware and software, did not become obsolete by the time the project was launched. A number of implementation problems, foreseen at the beginning of the implementation period, have arisen. The following strategies have been adopted to overcome these challenges:

Project approach: A project approach was followed from August 1997 to complete the project in a time-bound manner. For this purpose, the project was broken up into nine major tasks and 64 sub-tasks. A project report was prepared highlighting the action to be taken in respect of each task and sub-task and the responsibility for implementing each job. This was then communicated to all implementation agencies and selected field officers. The adoption of the project approach has brought the following benefits.

- The implementation agencies felt fully involved in the project.
- The implementation agencies were clear about the scope of the tasks to be accomplished in a stipulated time period.
- It was possible to start implementation of several tasks in parallel so that the project could be implemented in the minimum possible time.
- Each agency was aware of what the other agencies were doing; thus a team spirit could be built to decrease inevitable problems of coordination.

Procurement of hardware and system software: The hardware and system software required for the project was procured through the agency of AP Technology Services. About 2,000 items of hardware and peripherals and software packages were procured within a span of about five months.

Business process re-engineering: Computerization of the age-old process of registration called for considerable re-engineering effort. The more important results of this business process re-engineering effort are described shortly.

Amendment of the Registration Act: The Registration Act of 1908 is a legislation of the Union of India and does not provide for handling the registration process on computers. The Act together with the Rules and

Standing Orders provide in minute detail the manner of presentation of document, its scrutiny, the registration process, copying of the documents into volumes of books, the ink to be used for copying, etc. Copies of documents preserved in any other way would not have the legal sanction and so would not be admissible as evidence. To overcome this situation, the Registration Act, 1908, in its application to the state of AP has been amended to provide for the following:

- The process of registration of any category of documents may be completed and copying done with the help of electronic devices such as computers, scanners and CDs, and copies preserved and retrieved when required.
- Copies of documents registered and stored electronically, retrieved, printed and certified by the sub-registrar shall be received as evidence.
- The software to be used for registration shall be prescribed by the inspector general.

It took over a year for the amendment to become effective. The Government of AP notified 214 SROs, where the registration can be done using electronic devices. This amendment is effective from 5 February 1999.
Valuation of properties: This involves incorporating basic value guidelines into a master table of the computer and making the system compute the value of any property instantaneously without causing loss of revenue to the government or charging excess from the citizen. As a result,

- The procedure of spot inspection, which is often a discretionary process, has been dispensed with. It is replaced by a system of post-registration inspection of properties.
- The system of market value assistance across the counter is a direct offshoot of this effort.

Site preparation: The CARD project has attempted to radically improve the working environment, which involved the following:

- Standard designs for furnishing category A, B and C offices.
- Category A offices have been provided with air-conditioned environment with glass partitions and citizen counters.
- Standard plywood modular furniture was provided to category B and C sites.

- Concealed wiring and LAN cabling.
- All the CARD offices were given a facelift.

Training: To effectively use the technology, a well-designed, large training programme was implemented by NIIT (National Institute of Information Technology). Training was imparted to employees at five different levels.

Category	Number	Training period
Senior officers (DIGs and DRs)	45	1 week
Middle-level managers (ADRs)	50	3 weeks
Data processing officers (DPOs)	75	6 months
Sub-registrars	300	2 weeks
Data entry operators	1200	2 weeks

- The training programmes were implemented in a corporate-like environment at a cost of about $262,000 (Rs 1.13 crores).
- Decentralized training programmes were run at 25 centres in the state.
- Training course-ware was designed and supplied.
- The DPOs were groomed as technical resource persons at the district level, competent to install various kinds of software, trouble-shoot technically, and to transfer the skills required to manage the counters.

Extensive and far-reaching reforms in a system cannot be brought about without adequate motivation of the organization. Employees were motivated through the following steps:

- A cross-section of the field personnel was closely associated with the design and development of the software and especially in the task of business process re-engineering.
- No external technical personnel was recruited.
- The head of the department (the author) undertook extensive tours over the state and conducted workshops, presentations and special training camps involving all the employees of the department. The officials who managed the two pilot sites were closely associated with this effort.
- The acronym 'CARD' has contributed significantly to the identification of employees with the project.
- Support and association of senior functionaries of the government such as the principal secretary and minister of the revenue department have also been motivational factors.

Data backlog: The CARD masters (state level) could be built without much difficulty as the data is limited and is available. However, the project encountered major challenges in building up basic value data and EC data for the last 15 years. The basic value data, consisting of about 50,000 records at each SRO, was entered into the systems by the trained staff in six to eight weeks. While building the database critical to the running of the CARD system, the staff was able to acquire some hands-on experience.

The task of entering EC data, which has a more complex size and structure—about 12 million records of 2 KB size each—has been outsourced to from five agencies in March 1998. The department had to face scores of problems in ensuring speed with quality of data entry. The problems involved enforcing standards in data definition, iterative data validation and coordination between departmental staff and the private agencies. ECs are now being issued to citizens in five minutes after searching more than 15 years of records at over 50 offices.

Installation issues: Installing of CARD application software in 212 locations was considered a major problem. Seven versions of the software had to be developed, tested and deployed in a limited timeframe of four months to achieve desired functionality across the counter. This challenging task was made possible by the relentless efforts of the DPOs who were groomed in anticipation of this task. One significant strategy adopted to 'de-bottleneck' this process was to enable the DPOs to contact the head of department and a core of technical personnel at the headquarters at any time to solve problems encountered in installation.

Funding: The CARD project was funded entirely by the Government of AP. The original outlay was about US$3 million (Rs 13 crores). It is likely to grow to $4.3 million (Rs 18.5 crores) when final accounts are drawn. This would include hardware, software, training, site preparation, data entry, airconditioners, furniture, stationery and storage media, CARD software training and other miscellaneous expenses.

■ Launch of the CARD Project

CARD is one of the major IT projects undertaken by the Government of AP. Its success depends on the extent of awareness created among the registering public and on the ease, facility, speed and transparency of the CARD system. The CARD project was launched on 4 November 1998. All the centres were inaugurated on the same day by public representatives of that area. An appropriate media campaign was also simultaneously undertaken that made a definite impact not only in AP but all over India in the days and weeks that followed. It is necessary to continue the awareness campaign so that the domination and role of middlemen and brokers in the registration sector is eliminated.

It was forecast that the CARD project would need three months after the launch to stabilize. The complexity of the system, need for enough experience on the job, rectification of problems of hardware and software at some places are the factors necessitating a period of stabilization and transition from the manual to the computerized system.

After about six months of operation of the project, the results are found to be highly encouraging. About 80 per cent of all transactions are now done through CARD. Some of the transactions are still being handled manually at a few places due to hardware and software related problems. During the period of stabilization, the manual system of copying the indexing of documents was continued along with the computerized process. This has put unavoidable additional burden on the staff. The results achieved during the period from 4 November 1998 to 31 May 1999 are as shown:

Market value checkslips	164,231
Registrations	234,499
Value of stamps sold	Rs 740 million.

■ Plan to Sustain Operations

To sustain the CARD system, a transaction-based fee structure linked to the various registration services has been proposed, which is under consideration of the Government of AP. Under this scheme, a nominal fee would be charged for each transaction/service across the counter. The amount collected would be pooled at the district level—without having to remit to a government treasury—to meet expenditures towards stationery and media, maintenance of the equipment, electricity charges, software upgradation, etc.

Above all, a continuous public awareness campaign and the enforcement of a citizen's charter, which lays down service standards, should

■ Road Map

The CARD system replaces the existing manual services with computerized services besides introducing a few new services. This is the first step on the road to an ever-expanding world of exploitating information technology to improve citizen services. The following plans are being contemplated.

- Introduction of a Telugu version of the software.
- Establishing a CARD service centre that provides all registration related services, except registration of deeds, relating to any property in the twin cities under one roof.
- Networking all the servers/PCs at 214 centres using the AP State Wide Area Network (APSWAN) so that all registration services, except registration of deeds, can be accessed at any of the 214 offices irrespective of location of property.
- Providing registration information services on the Internet.
- Development of a property title database, which would be the precursor for introducing the Torrens system of registration (whereby registration of a sale deed guarantees title to a property).
- Linking up of databases of all land-related departments such as land revenue, municipal administration and irrigation.
- Linking up the EC database with banking network to facilitate speedier processing of applications for rural credit.

■ Future Beneficiaries

There is a strong likelihood that the project will make a dent in the operations of brokers and middlemen, and reduce corrupt practices. Since 60 per cent of the documents, ECs and certified copies relate to agricultural properties, the CARD project will help the rural farming community. Agriculturists would also benefit from a possible link-up of the CARD network with the rural bank network, which enhances the efficiencies of rural credit services by eliminating the need for paper medium.

■ Replication of CARD in Other States

The Registration Act 1908 is a Central Act, so the procedures are almost the same throughout the country. Therefore, it should be feasible to replicate the reforms brought about through the CARD project in AP in other states with suitable customization appropriate to local situations. However, it is essential to recognize that the respective states have to make concerted efforts to put the enablers in position to ensure successful replication within a limited timeframe.

■ Conclusion

This paper has described the concept and implementation of computerizing and reforming a department with a large public interface. The CARD project ensures speedy, transparent, easily accessible and reliable services to citizens. Initial results indicate a good possibility of the project shaping into an extremely citizen-friendly application with prospects of further improvements and replication in other states.

Notes

1. Copies of registration documents certified by sub-registrars are often required by litigants to be produced before the courts. It involves retrieving the copy of the original document from the relevant volume kept in the record room of the sub-registrar office (SRO). Copying it is done manually, comparing with the volume to edit mistakes, attesting and delivering to the applicant is laborious and time-consuming.
2. An Encumbrance Certificate (EC) is a document listing the transactions that occurred in relation to a property over a period preceding the date of application for such certificate. It is required by financial institutions before granting a loan on mortgage of a property as also by prospective purchasers of property to ascertain the nature of charges on the property. ECs are typically sought for the preceding 13 years (12 years being the period for getting title by adverse possession). It involves manual search of the indexes and volumes relating to the preceding 13 years.

Annexure

Hardware and Software used in CARD project

SERVER: IBM Net Infinity 3,500 PC-based server
Intel Pentium Mhz with 32 bit PCI bus
64 MB SD RAM ECC DIMM expandable to 512 MB
2 × 4.33 GB Ultra Fast SCSI-II HDD
1 × 600 MB IDE CD-ROM with 24x speed
14" SVGA mono monitor
32 bit ethernet card, 33.6 kbps data/fax internal modem

CLIENT: Pentium Clients with Intel Pentium CPU @ 166 Mhz MMX, PC/ISA Bus
2 × 168 pin DIMM slots
32 MB SD RAM expandable to 128 MB
2 × 2.0 GB SCSI Hard disk drive with PCI-SCSI controller
HP T 41(4/8GB) SCSI CTD (3.5")
15" SVGA colour monitor
Gist card with GIST firmware ver 8.041
32 bit ethernet card with UTP and BNC ports

SCANNER: A4 size SCANNER with ADF (50 pages capacity)
(Flat bet, colour 600 dpi, speed=8 sec/per text page @ 300 dpi)

Laser printer: Printing speed upto 8 ppm, Printing resolution: 600*600 dpi
Buffer capacity: 2 M byte expandable to M byte
Printer language: Windows compatible
Interface: Parallel, Paper size: A4 size, letter, executive
Power supply: 220V, 50 HZ
Paper tray capacity: 100 sheets
Paper types: Plain paper, envelopes, transparency
Consumables: Toner cartridges

CD Writer: 6X read 2X write external drive with SCSI interface
With append mode writing CD WRITER with SCSI Port

The following combination of software packages has been chosen.

A & B Categories

OS for the server SCO UNIX Version 5.04
OS for the client Windows '95 Version 4.00
RDBMS Oracle work group server

Version 7.3, 2, 2.0
Front-end for the clients Developer 2,000 Forms - 4.5
Reports - 2.5

C Category

Operating System Windows '95 Version 4.00
RDBMS Personal Oracle Version 7.3, 2, 2.0
Front-end Developer 2,000 Forms - 4.5
Reports - 2.5

Imaging software: A customized scanning software was developed with all the security and other features required by the CARD project. The salient features of the imaging software developed are as follows:

1. Scanning of only the registered documents.
2. Archiving of images of documents on to CD/tape.
3. Retrieval of the documents by document identifier.
4. Audit trail.
5. Management reports on documents scanned.
6. Online help feature.

6

Computerization of *Mandal* Revenue Offices in Andhra Pradesh: Integrated Certificate Application

ASOK KUMAR

Information and communication technologies are important tools of the Government of Andhra Pradesh to become SMART (simple, moral, accountable, responsive and transparent). Andhra Pradesh is the first state in India to design a statewide computerization programme covering all levels of the administrative spectrum from the smallest—the *Mandal* Revenue Offices (MROs)—to the highest, largest and most powerful. This paper presents a review of the computerization programme of the 1,124 MROs in the state and its first application—the delivery of statutory certificates stating caste, place and date of birth, and landholding to individuals in a few minutes without the current delay of 20 to 30 days.

■ Introduction

The Government of Andhra Pradesh (AP) plans to introduce computers at all levels of state administration to improve citizen services. The government has consolidated computerization and provision of technical services into a separate department. AP was ahead of other states in creating a citizen's database. The Statewide Multi-Purpose Household Survey (MPHS) was launched in 1995. It is being used to store large volumes of data—information useful to make quick, transparent and objective decisions and to cut bureaucratic delays at various levels. Other uses include analysis of citizen data and information exchange through networking. All high profile IT initiatives in the state are largely the result of Chief Minister N. Chandrababu Naidu's vision and determination. Political leadership is particularly important for cross-departmental IT projects.

With the large Andhra Pradesh Secretariat Campus Network at one end of the spectrum and the *mandals* (lowermost institutionalized tier of the state administration) at the other end, the MRO project envisages introducing computers right down to the *mandal* level. For the Andhra Pradesh Statewide Area Network (APSWAN), a 2 MBP optic fibre link would connect the state secretariat with 23 district headquarters and serve as the backbone for 'multi-services' (voice, video and data). These multi-services would improve coordination between state headquarters and district offices in managing various regulatory, developmental and hazard mitigation programmes of the state government. They would also ensure quick, accurate and efficient aggregation of large amounts of data generated at the *mandal* levels for performance monitoring and analysis at both micro and macro levels.

■ The Set-up

Many villages constitute a *mandal*. There are 1,124 *mandals* in the state, each with a population ranging from 35,000 to 500,000. A group of seven to 15 *mandals* forms a revenue division. There are in all 78 revenue divisional offices in the state. One or more revenue divisions are grouped together to form 23 districts.

■ The Scope

The scope of the project is to computerize all the MROs (1,124), revenue divisional offices (78), collectorates at state headquarters (23), office of the commissioner of land revenue, directorate of economics and statistics and the central headquarters in Hyderabad. The two-year computerization project would include data collection, coordinating the implementation of different databases and developing human resources through intensive training. Funding for the computerization of the *mandals* is part of a World Bank Hazard Mitigation and Emergency Cyclone Recovery Project, which supports the government's efforts to improve data collection and communication of relevant hazard and vulnerability reduction information from the district and *mandal* level to citizens.

In MRO offices, apart from land records and data from the MPHS, there are large volumes of data relating to the Public Distribution System (PDS), elections, and flood and cyclone management. The MPHS data include socio-economic details of all citizens living in the *mandal*. In addition, it has a large amount of data that is generated periodically at village/*mandal* level through surveys and in departmental monitoring forms.

The scope of the project for all *mandal* offices, includes procurement and installation of necessary hardware and software; field verification, validation and updating of the MPHS database; development and installation of various software applications; development of IT human resources through extensive training on computers, general and application software to 5,000 MRO staff; and assignment of unique identification numbers to all citizens in the state.

There are three categories of work to be automated.

Category I (work process to be computerized)
- Issue of integrated certificates (which have details of caste, place and date of birth), birth and death certificates, income certificates, pensions, ration cards, reports and periodicals.
- Maintenance of village revenue records, *patta*[1] transfers, management of revenue demands, management of government/surplus lands.

Category II (manual work processes monitored on computer)
- Assignment of government/surplus lands, land acquisition, collection of revenues, monitoring of public grievance, court cases, welfare schemes, hazard mitigation, planning relief and rescue operations, and disbursing compensation.
- Monitoring the performance of every employee of the state government.
- Statistical information on landholding census, crop particulars, weather and climate, livestock census, economic census, population census, irrigation surveys, house building and agricultural wages.

Category III (back-office functions to be computerized)
- All personnel registers, registers under the District Office Manual (DOM), payrolls and 22 registers recording cash transactions.

■ Technology Used

In accordance with the IT policy of the state, a client–server architecture has been adopted in the project. Every MRO will have at least one server and two client PCs with adequate power to process data and support data mining capabilities envisaged in the APSWAN project. This would mean approximately 1,400 servers and 2,500 client PCs. At the headquarter level it is proposed to have PCs for faster processing and handling geographical information system (GIS) data, while those at the *mandals* will be used for data entry and information lookup. Since at present APSWAN extends only to the districts, dial-up modems are to be used to access data located in remote MRO offices. Figure 6.1 provides an overview of the technical configuration, including wide area network (APSWAN) at the state and district levels and campus local area network (LAN) to be established in public offices.

■ Integrated Certificates

The first phase targets issuing integrated certificates across a counter to citizens from the MROs. A view of a citizen–customer interface counter can be seen in Figure 6.2. The certificates will be based on a validated

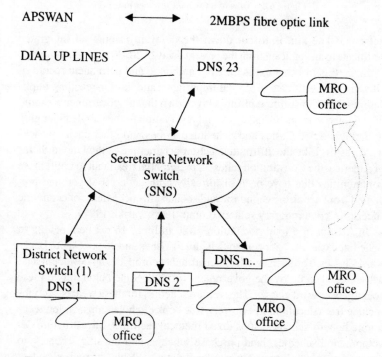

Figure 6.1 Functional Diagram of the APSWAN (AP State Wide Area Network)

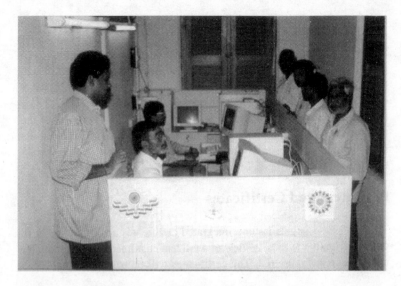

Figure 6.2   View of a Citizen Customer Interface

database. The aim is to cut down the delay in issuing an integrated certificate to an applicant from the present delay of 20–30 days to 10 minutes.

Since this information is the only authentic and permanent record of citizens, the certificate is of vital importance and has far-reaching implications. The Constitution of India lays down that all governments should take proactive steps to ensure special reservation to the people belonging to the Scheduled Castes and Scheduled Tribes and other socially backward castes. Like the affirmative action programme in the United States of America, the Constitution relies on preferential treatment to uplift those communities that have been historically both underprivileged and prevented from acquiring economic and social skills necessary for economic success in contemporary society (Gupta 1998; Parikh 1997).

In AP, out of a total population of 80 million, 16 per cent belong to Scheduled Castes, 7 per cent to Scheduled Tribes and 36 per cent to Backward Classes. The social welfare department coordinates all developmental activities taken up by the government for the people belonging to these socially backward classes. The welfare schemes for these weaker sections include free education, free hostels, free books, scholarships, various economic benefit schemes, subsidized medical facilities, infrastructure developmental schemes, land purchase schemes and housing schemes, to name a few. According to the tentative figures available, the revised budget of the implementing department was a whopping $18,940,000 approximately (Rs 81.5 crores) in 1997–98 and is estimated to go up to $20,070,000 (Rs 86.32 crores) in 1998–99! Integrated certificates containing caste particulars are necessary for a person to avail such benefits. This further underlines the importance and implication of integrated certificates.

■ Implementation

Implementation of the project is being phased keeping in mind the absorptive capacity of the administrative system and the vastness of the scope of the project—both geographical and technological. A pilot study was initiated in Moinabad *mandal* of Ranga Reddy district in April 1998. In the first phase of the project in August 1998, computers were introduced in another 90 MROs, located at the headquarters of revenue divisional offices that were spread over 23 districts. This covered most of the urban areas of the state and hence a substantial population. In the second phase, the remaining 230 MROs located at the headquarters of the erstwhile *talukas*[2] will be taken up.

■ Capability Building

For proper use of this technology, computer training had to be imparted to the staff of the MROs. Two operators (at the level of junior assistants) and two system administrators (at the level of senior assistants) were given training for periods varying from 10 days to 20 days in the operation of computers and application software. In addition, a few persons from the office of the collector were also given training. A total of about 410 persons have been trained under phase I.

Intensive training for a period of one month was imparted to four persons, identified from each district as district resources persons (DRPs). Thus a total of 92 well-trained personnel assists the implementation of the project at the district level. Periodic refresher courses are also organized for them.

Capability building has now to be undertaken for another 4,000 persons. The training, based on a well-developed training syllabus, will be conducted at the district level by reputed training institutions.

■ Data Validation

Before actually using the voluminous MPHS data collected in 1995, it had to be verified and re-validated at the field level. After the teams of revenue department staff completed these verifications, the MRO certified the entire database.

■ Process Re-engineering: The Existing Set-up Versus the New Set-up

In the existing set-up, a person requiring a certificate of his/her caste or date of birth has to apply in writing to the competent authority in form I or II, prescribed in Government Order (GO) No. 58, SW (J), 12 May 1997. The *mandal* revenue officer marks it to the revenue inspector, who in turn authorizes the village administrative officer (VAO) for inquiry. After the inquiry, if the VAO is satisfied about the claim of the applicant, he recommends issue of the certificate. The revenue inspector countersigns this recommendation. On receipt of the recommendation, the *mandal* revenue officer marks the application to the clerk concerned, who fills in the relevant columns in the pre-printed integrated certificate. This certificate is numbered, entered in a register and sent to the *mandal* revenue officer for his signature. He signs the certificate and affixes his seal, and the certificate is then given to the applicant after taking an acknowledgement receipt. This process takes between 20 to 30 days.

Under the new set-up, the applicant will apply for the integrated certificate in the prescribed form at the citizen interface counter. The junior assistant/operator will number it and ascertain the correctness of the claim by checking with the validated and certified database in the computer. The authorized person/competent person will print out the certificate on the computer. The certificate issued by the computer will not only be exactly similar to the format given in the relevant GO but will also have a bar code to check its authenticity. The whole process will take less than 15 minutes.

The *mandal* revenue officer continues to be the authorized/competent person. It has now been suggested that since the entire database is to be certified by the competent person, the superintendent of the MRO (who is of the rank of the deputy *tehasildar*[3]) be a resident officer available in the office at all times. This avoids unnecessary delay in the issue of certificates in case the officer is unavailable.

■ Site Preparation

In all the MROs, minor civil and electrical works were required to ensure a decent building, electrical connectivity and grounding. MROs under phase I were provided with a uniformly and aesthetically designed citizen interface counter to bring about an improvement in the environment and work culture. This is intended to reduce the difficulties people face in having to go to various sections in the MRO to obtain services. It also reduces the level of corruption.

■ Security of Data and Audit Trail

In addition to keeping track of all the certificates issued, it is also mandatory to keep a record of the people who process the requisition, who authorize it, and who finally hand over the printed certificate. The software designed has the necessary facilities to capture the 'electronic signature' of the personnel handling these facilities. Access to the database is controlled by the authorized personnel and would be thus read-only, with special provision for alteration.

■ Unique Identity Number

Each person in the database will have an individual identity number. This would be referred to as the Social Security Identification (SSID) number. This number will be a 16 digit code, where the first two digits will represent the state, the next two the district, followed by the *mandal*, the village/ward, the household number, and the last serial number will be of the person in the household survey data. The SSID will be electronically transferred from one *mandal* to another in case an individual shifts his/her residence within the state.

■ Implementation Challenges

Problems Related to Data

Compiling a cross-departmental data posed major impediments that had to be overcome.

- Since the data was collected three years ago, most of it had to be re-validated. This was done by teams of revenue department staff (since this data is in the custody of the revenue department and only they are empowered to make changes).
- There were no uniform standard codes in 1995 for the districts, *mandals* or villages, and for castes at the time of data entry. This created difficulties in accessing the correct data. Now, all codes have been standardized and their use has been made mandatory to all departments by a government order. This will facilitate exchange of information throughout the state, between departments at different levels.

Poor Infrastructure Facilities

Of the 1,124 MROs, 628 are located in government buildings and 496 in private buildings that have been rented. Many of these buildings are in bad shape and require repair. In many offices electrical wiring is unsatisfactory and in most cases grounding is not provided which is a pre-requisite for trouble-free functioning of computers.

Vastness of Scope — Geographical and Technological

Approximately 4,500 computers along with related accessories such as printers, UPS and monitors are to be installed in 1,124 MROs in 23 districts spread over an area of 275,045 sq. km. The large scope and the vastness of the geographical area has created a need for extra resources to procure, deploy, operate and maintain the large number of computers. This in turn has presented difficulties in project management as a single unit in Hyderabad has to cater to all these demands.

Lack of Trained Human Resources

Another major challenge is the lack of human resources in terms of computer literate staff and absorption abilities for over 5,000 MROs. It was estimated that training 5,000 people as computer operators at the district level at a man–machine ratio of 1:1 would take approximately six months. To prevent 'vaporizing' of the skills acquired, the timing of training and procurement and installation of computers need to be synchronized.

Coordination with Various Departments

Establishing and maintaining project interfaces is an essential factor in the success of large, complex IT projects. In this project, activities are intermeshed with previously undertaken projects and with other ongoing projects. Clear governance of the interrelationships and coordination responsibilities among areas for delivery of application software requires a lot of communication from other departments and agencies, e.g., the MPHS database is handled by the revenue department, the Hazard Mitigation Information System (HMIS) is handled by the disaster management unit of the finance and planning department and commissioner, relief; land records are managed by the National Informatics Centre (NIC) and the revenue department; and the civil supplies database is handled by the civil supplies department. The social welfare department frames the rules for the issue of integrated certificates given by the MROs of the revenue department. There is only one project director, with a limited number of supporting staff to ensure the implementation of this complex project cutting across various departments of the government. However, there is a high-level Domain Expert Committee and State-level Committee on Computerization of Land Records to provide guidance. Andhra Pradesh Technological Services (APTS) assist the project director in the technical component of the project, including the procurement of hardware, software and integration of modules from relevant departments and specialized agencies.

Work Culture

Though the revenue department provides an impetus to all other departments, it is steeped in traditions, antiquated procedures and protocols, thus making it difficult to adopt innovations, such as the use of information technology. Persistent motivation and capacity building exercises are required to bring about this change especially at the initial stages. The process of demystification of computer technology has already started in all the phase I *mandals.*

■ Implementation Results and Benefits

Information technology has been successfully introduced in phase I MROs (90) for the issue of integrated caste certificates. Data has been re-validated and the staff trained. Citizen interface counters have been set up.

Application software has been identified and pilot studies are being conducted. The actual impact would be felt when the season for the requirement of the certificates sets in. The certificates are mainly issued to students belonging to socially backward classes at the start of the academic year, i.e., in the months of April through July, to obtain the benefits of the reservation policy. Phase II has already been initiated. A complementary land records package has been implemented in selected *mandal*s of Ranga Reddy district.

This project is part of an overall AP government strategy and there are many other sub-projects coming up. This assures some certainty in terms of correctness of the implementation against a moving, larger target. Since this project is in the embryonic stage, extrapolation of progress against milestones and cost incurred at this time might not produce the required results.

■ Conclusion

The IT application project described here is very challenging both in terms of delivery and support. It is a complex operation, requiring coordination with various departments at different levels. There are very few examples of such a project in rural areas of any other developing country. The installation of over 4,500 computers for over 80 million records in the MPHS database, developing customized software applications for diverse departments, and providing computer training to over 5,000 staff is a very daunting set of tasks. But long marches start with small steps—steady, confident and one at a time.

Notes

1. A *patta* is a document establishing an individual's right of possession to land.
2. A *taluka* is the same as a *tehasil* in other states and a *mandal* in Andhra Pradesh. It is a unit of administration above the village and below a sub-division.
3. A *tehasildar* is the officer in charge of a *tehasil/taluka*. In Andhra Pradesh he/she is known as the *mandal* revenue officer.

References

Gupta, D., 1998, A Question of Quota. *Seminar*, No. 471, November, pp. 57–62.
Parikh, S., 1997, The Politics of Preference: Democratic Institutions and Affirmative Action in the United States and India. University of Michigan Press, Ann Arbor, Michigan, pp. 172–75.

7

Application of Information Technology for Rural Postal System

MAJOR RAMAKRISHNAN

The village postmaster, teacher and health worker, who work as group leaders, play an important role in rural development. Although the relationship between these people and villagers has been strengthened over a period of time through primary contact, these interactions could be better. Information technology can be used in optimizing their regular work schedules, thus saving time for these informal interactions. We have found that when there is time for these relationships to develop, the economic status of the villagers improves. CMC has designed and built a compact portable and user-friendly embedded system called CUPS (Computerized Universal Postal System). This system meets all the Indian postal requirements, works either alone or in a network, and can also work on solar power in rural areas. A weighing machine has been integrated with the system to improve its compactness and utility. These machines have been tried in and around Hyderabad.

■ Introduction

The use of information technology in postal services aims at improving productivity, improving services to the customer, ensuring proper accounting of transactions, generating necessary MIS reports, and fruitfully utilizing the time of the postmasters.

Along with village teachers and healthcare workers, the village postmaster constantly interacts with the local community. These people play an important role in the socio-economic development of the rural masses but their work time is burdened with overwhelming paperwork responsibilities, which affect their ability to interact with the citizens they serve.

There are 150,000 post offices in the country, of which about 25,000 are departmental sub-post offices. In the Eighth Five Year Plan, about 800 post offices were computerized by installing multipurpose counter machines. Unless a massive computerization programme is launched, it will take decades before there is widespread deployment of IT to improve both productivity and services to citizens in post offices. So it becomes imperative to exploit existing technology to the fullest (Indiresan 1999; Vittal 1997). CMC took up the development of an embedded system for the postal department taking into account the requirements for rural use.

With the infrastructure available, it is important to specifically design systems to suit the existing environment. The use of PCs in urban areas cannot be readily extended to rural areas due to lack of connectivity, inadequate power, and non-availability of skilled manpower for maintenance. The need is to develop a system that can work in a rural environment. The system should be highly reliable, tamper-proof, compact and portable, user-friendly, able to operate in stand alone as well as in networking mode, and operate in harsh and remote environments.

■ Technology Used

Based on the aforesaid requirements, CMC has developed and designed an exclusive machine for the postal department called CUPS (Computerized Universal Postal System).

Design Considerations

The equipment had to be designed such that it ideally never fails, and in case of failure, the parts should be so cheap that they can be dispensed with and replaced with new ones. In case the parts are indispensable they should be easily repairable.

Despite the strides that have been made in quality assurance and reliability controls, there is still a need to cope with problems of system failure (Siegal 1964, 1969). Taking into account the large increase in the number of functions in new computer systems, a higher density of functional and physical packaging of new systems requiring more refined processing techniques and controls, it is practically impossible to have a fail-proof system. It is therefore advisable to have a 'reasonable' amount of reliability because the reliability cost after a certain level shoots up exponentially as is seen from the graph in Figure 7.1.

With a reasonable amount of reliability, considering the reliability cost and a good level of maintainability, equipment can be repaired in the shortest possible time.

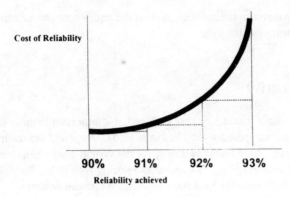

Figure 7.1   Cost of Reliability

Thus a high level of availability can be achieved at an economic cost of improved maintainability. The overall cost comprising cost of reliability and cost of failure is shown in Figure 7.2. Figure 7.3 indicates how the inclusion of cost of maintainability brings down the total cost considerably, thus, having a lesser cost for the same level of availability.

To increase the level of reliability, failure prone components such as floppy and hard disks were dispensed with and an embedded system meeting the requirements of the postal system was designed. The embedded system eliminates the virus proneness of the PC, reduces overhead costs and ensures response times without human errors. The components are arranged in the mother-board for easy accessibility. Built-in diagnosis

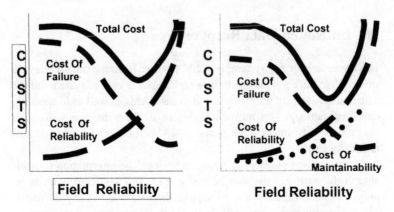

Figure 7.2   Cost of Reliability and Failure

Figure 7.3   Cost of Reliability and Failure with Maintainability

is incorporated in the software so that the equipment can be repaired in the shortest possible time.

■ Security

Since financial transactions are involved, it is important to make sure that they are not tampered with. The embedded concept and the security features ensure a high level of security for the system even when operated in remote, harsh environments where monitoring is difficult. The following four levels of security have been introduced into the system.

- **Physical security**: Lock and key have been provided for basic security.
- **Logical security**: User-id, password and special privileged operations are important features of logical security. The supervisor can override the privileges given to the operator at the counter, depending on the operational requirements.
- **Data security**: Data can be stored in a battery backed RAM and can be retained even in case of power failure. This is done without any floppy or hard disk to minimize the corruption of data.
- **Software security**: Software security has been ensured by storing the application software in EPROMS and developing an exclusive operating system. This ensures that the output is not tampered with.

■ Improved Data Recovery

It is important for any system, especially where financial transactions are involved, to have a provision to recover the data in case of system failure. The transactions are normally stored in the RAMs as well as in specially designed cartridges for mirror imaging of all the transactions stored in the main RAMs. Information stored in RAMs is battery backed and thus not easily lost.

In case of any problem in the main system, the information is available in the cartridge that can be easily read. The data cartridge can be plugged into another system to retrieve the data without any difficulty. This is very important especially in rural areas where immediate maintenance support is not readily available.

■ Easy Tariff Change

In India, tariffs are usually modified every year. Modifying the tariffs at different places within a short period of time is quite difficult. When equipment is spread out over wide geographical areas, the design of the software should ensure that present as well as new tariffs are stored in the cartridge. New tariffs can thus be easily introduced into the system before the effective date of implementing new tariffs. The old tariffs as well as the new tariffs can be stored in the cartridge and sent to different locations before the implementation date. The software will instantaneously switch over to the new tariff when required.

■ Adaptability to Networking

CUPS can be operated on a stand alone basis and can be networked with other similar machines as well as to a host machine. When it operates as a stand alone, it can create its own MIS reports; when networked, it can transfer data from individual machines to a Centralized Accounting and Reporting System (CARS) machine for all accounting purposes and for generation of reports required by the postal department.

■ Easy Interface with Any System

This system has user-friendly prompts and messages to help postal employees operate it. There are keys for frequently used transactions with automatic time-stamping and report generation at the end of the shift. The exclusive display to the customer indicates the cost incurred in a particular transaction, thus involving the customer in the process. The printing, scanning and recording of bar-codes improves the functional capability in tracking packages. To make the system compact, a weighing machine is also interfaced using the same system processor. This brings down the cost of the equipment and makes it easily affordable.

■ Architecture

To meet the functional requirements in a harsh environment, the system is based on rugged hardware to achieve a high level of reliability. This unique system consists of a proprietary hardware based on Motorola 68K processor. It has 256K of PROM and 128K of battery backed RAM. The dialogue with the operator is through an 8 × 40 column LCD (Liquid Crystal Display) and a normal QWERTY keyboard. A five column 7 segment LED display is provided for displaying commission/time to the customer. A special transaction cartridge is provided which consists of 64K of PROM and 64K of battery backed RAM. A high speed dot matrix printer is used to print receipts.

The pluggable cartridge improves data recovery, the battery backed RAMs help to store the data in case of power failures, and its compact size facilitates transportation of equipment. In case of power failures, the specifically designed operating system makes the equipment fully operational in a short time. For rural areas, it is designed to operate with solar power. A photograph of CUPS machine is shown in Figure 7.4.

■ Functionality

The system can handle different functions of a post office from a single counter. The functions include money orders, registered articles, parcels, speed post, inland/overseas mail, unclassified receipts, telegraphic receipts, value paid articles and postal life insurance.

Figure 7.4 The CUPS machine

■ Centralized Accounting and Reporting System (CARS)

To improve accounting procedures and generate accounting reports in post offices, where the number of counters is large, a PC-based accounting system called CARS is attached to the existing CUPS machine. CARS generates a consolidated report of all transactions carried out by the CUPS machine. Once data from a CUPS machine is successfully transferred to a CARS PC, the same procedure can be run to generate various types of reports. All the necessary security aspects are also taken care of by the software of the CARS machine. Normally, the software runs on WINDOWS NT with the necessary user-friendly graphical interface. Menus assist even a non-computer literate operator to carry out his tasks easily. These machines have been put to trial testing in three locations around Hyderabad (Himmathnagar, High Court and Golconda post offices) for a period of six months. There has been positive feedback about the versatility of the machines in postal applications.

■ Conclusion

CUPS is a tailor-made system exclusively designed and developed by CMC to be used by the department of post as a comprehensive solution to meet its requirements even in rural areas. These machines are capable of issuing various receipts from a single counter. In case of post offices having more than one counter, each of these machines can be connected to a centralized PC that will perform all the accounting and report generation. The embedded architecture provides necessary security and facilitates operation in remote locations. The system can be hooked up with communication links to larger post offices for better communication.

The use of information technology has benefited the customer by having general purpose counters, where all types of transactions can be done at one counter. Thus there is considerable reduction in waiting time. Moreover, the customer is kept directly involved as the money to be paid is displayed on the board. The system can also incorporate regional languages for improving the user-friendliness of the product.

The operating staff is also benefited by the generation of an automatic summary report at the end of the shift that makes the winding up of a shift much simpler. This also facilitates easy accounting of transactions and cash. The saved time of the operator/postmaster especially in rural areas could be effectively utilized in educating villages in different areas such as health and education, which in turn would improve the literacy level. From the management point of view, one can have improved customer satisfaction, optimal utilization of resources, record keeping, and reduction of malpractices.

References

Indiresan, P.V., 1999, Seeds of Change. *The Hindu*, March 6.
Siegal, J. William, 1964, Fault Rectification in Maintenance System and Technology for Network Repair and Modification.
Vittal, N., 1969, Support of Modern Electronic Equipment: Facts or Fantasies.
————, 1997, Indian Post: Cinderella to Princess. *The Economic Times*, October 27.

PART IV

**Empowering Citizens through Access
to Information and Knowledge**

8

Knowledge Network for Recognizing, Respecting and Rewarding Grassroots Innovation

ANIL K. GUPTA, BRIJ KOTHARI AND KIRIT PATEL

Barriers of literacy, localism and language impede lateral learning among creative communities. The inability of formal science and technology institutions to add value to local innovations further reduces the potential that grassroots green innovations may have in making a society more sustainable. Conventional, textual and printed information-based knowledge networks created by the Honey Bee Network have helped create a community of interested stakeholders building bridges between formal and informal knowledge systems. This paper[1] describes the use of multimedia and multi-language Honey Bee database in overcoming some of the constraints of conventional knowledge networks. It shows how the Honey Bee Network database—developed by the Society for Research and Initiatives for Sustainable Technologies and Institutions (SRISTI)—can influence public policy so that local communities and individual innovators are empowered and enabled to learn from each other across large spatial distances, languages and cultures; without being literate.

■ Introduction

The decline of the welfare state in the developed world has in recent times been accompanied with the denial or 'unfeasibility' of similar pursuits in developing countries. Squeezed by structural reforms, a lack of new social imagination is as much a commentary on the state of our civic consciousness as it is on the fragility and bankruptcy of our intellectual apparatus drawn from the legacy of the Marshal Plan and 'do gooding' state bureaucracies. We now need a new paradigm of envisioning social change and development built around overcoming information asymmetries. Knowledge can become a means of power if coalitions or networks of relevant actors evolve. The chemistry of evolution of such networks, which connect information, institutions and incentives with innovations and enterprises, is the subject of this paper.

The French philosopher, Abbe Pierre, argued that modern (read 'Western') society is confronted with three realities. The first pertains to the growing power of media and travelling which deny civilized society an excuse of not knowing; the second deals with the obligation of developed countries to deal with the rising problems of unemployment by reducing working hours; and the third refers to the challenge of utilizing enormous free time. We argue in this paper that every time information and communication technology (ICT) reduces information asymmetries, it can also help increase responsibility. One can no more make an excuse of not knowing for non-intervention since, as we illustrate with the example of a knowledge network/centre approach to augment grassroots creativity, ICT also helps align key actors in civil society. The alienation, fragmentation and dislocation of knowledge space make it difficult for creative urges of society at the grassroots level to coalesce. Market forces, as these have evolved, are generally successful in bringing together certain interests at specific scales. However, market failure is evident when transaction costs are high. Investment in ICT infrastructure can help to reduce these transaction costs for those whose ability to pay for them is low. But this will not happen automatically. Just as paving roads in forests often leads to accelerated deforestation[2] (Patel and Madhavan 1984), ICT infrastructure can lead to quick erosion of local knowledge and wisdom unless appropriate institutional interventions are made simultaneously.

■ Legacy of Development

The developmental paradigm has been dominated for at least half a century by the idea that the role of state or civil society is to provide the poor with material resources, with opportunities for skill or income augmentation and with employment. Strategies have never been built upon a resource in which poor people are often rich, i.e., their knowledge. Indeed developmental lexicon in the last decade adopted a term with great alacrity— 'resource poor people', assuming that 'knowledge' is not a resource. This blemish can be traced in almost every major developmental writing. Once knowledge is recognized as the fundamental building block of developmental options for disadvantaged communities around the world, the role of ICT becomes conspicuous in this envisioning process.

■ Incentives and ICT

Information and communication technology can be harnessed to generate incentives for knowledge-rich but economically poor people to share their knowledge without exhausting their Intellectual Property Rights (IPRs) and without creating fear of being robbed of their only resource. This can be done by providing a global registration system such as International Network for Sustainable Technological Applications and Registration (INSTAR) that will be discussed shortly. ICT can also hold together institutions for conservation, particularly, when the need for horizontal flow of information among communities facing different challenges is very high.

The greater the specificity of environmental challenges, the more likely it is that local knowledge systems will be isolated and fragmented. And yet analogic learning systems thrive precisely on such dissimilarities and discontinuities of knowledge systems. Fragmentation of knowledge space takes place due to various social divisions and cleavages, discontinuities in inter-generational transfer of traditional functional knowledge, and incommensurability between knowledge and the accompanying ecological and other resource contexts. Fragmentation can also arise if contemporary innovations for resource use are not shared widely. This may either be due to the dominance of external knowledge systems or due to contempt for local and familiar knowledge as happens in many communities and societies. The analogic learning can help overcome many of these discontinuities by helping: (*a*) search for solutions in different contexts; (*b*) provide clues about the kind of relationships that can be pursued; and (*c*) enrich the repertoire of local communities and innovators so that they can independently locate ideas for solutions as well as alternative materials. The basic idea of such analogic learning systems, is, for example, that even if fish are not found in dry regions, knowledge about another community using plants to numb fish before catching them, may trigger some other uses of toxic plants in a pastoral community, say, for veterinary medicine.

■ Some Observations

While ICT can provide a mechanism to abstract and exchange information on the heuristics underlying innovations, it has its limitations. For instance, the ethical values which encourage sharing of knowledge at the local level are also accompanied by general contempt or indifference towards local innovations in many societies. This paper provides some practical ways in which low cost ICT applications have provided incentives for sharing local innovations and establishing institutional mechanisms for the production, reproduction, exchange and critical (but appreciative) peer evaluation of knowledge systems for sustainable resource use.

Knowledge systems that enable people to survive, particularly in high risk environments, have involved blending the secular with the sacred, reductionism with holism, short-term options with long-term ones, specialized with diversified strategies; involving individual or collective material or non-material pursuits. Classical dichotomous approaches have seldom worked. The environmental ethic of these communities have also reflected these blends contrary to the populist rhetoric of so-called unitary approaches with one kind of strategies, for instance, holistic strategies dominating and displacing reductionist ones.

The higher the stress—whether physical, technological, market, or socio-economic—the greater the probability that disadvantaged communities and individuals will generate innovative and creative alternatives for resource use. Innovations, whether originating in traditional or contemporary consciousness, can develop from communities as well as from individuals. An overemphasis on community development to the exclusion of contribution of individuals may have lead to widespread indifference towards tapping the potential of knowledge rich economically poor people.

The ICT needs in areas where the majority of households are managed by women will be quite different from those dominated by male decision makers. The health needs, agricultural systems, technological challenges and interface between cultural taboos and economic pressures are most acute in these areas. Knowledge networks can generate new choices by connecting one group of women, who may have overcome some socio-cultural contraints to their economic improvement, with another group that is struggling to do so.

ICT can either help bridge or widen the gap between haves and have-nots. What is encouraging about the new possibilities that ICT trends offer is the scope for democratizing knowledge. Work done at IIMA has demonstrated how administrative systems can become transparent and citizens can benefit from easy access to information (Bhatnagar 1992, 1995; Bhatnagar et al. 1991; Kaul 1979a, 1979b, 1980, 1991; Patel and Madhavan 1977). The multimedia database conceptualized by SRISTI[3] (Society for Research and Initiatives for Sustainable Technologies and Institutions) and the Honey Bee Network demystifies the technology to empower local communities and innovators in rural areas. In the process it also democratizes knowledge through horizontal networking.

Finally, innovations in technological, cultural or institutional subsets often remain isolated and unconnected despite the existence of reasonably robust informal knowledge networks.

■ The Honey Bee Network and Multimedia Database

A knowledge network that connects innovators, enterprises and investments (see Figure 8.1) in an institutional context appears to be the most viable approach for future sustainable development. The points of departure for the Honey Bee Network, which began 10 years ago, were: first, we, the outsiders, should not make the poor complain when we take away their knowledge just as flowers do not when bees take away nectar; second, we should connect people to people as bees connect to other bees while pollinating. The genesis of the Honey Bee Network lies in a self-critical realization that the first author faced while looking at his own work drawing upon insights gained from creativity and innovation at the grassroots level until the mid-1980s. Anil K. Gupta had grown in his career but his accountability towards knowledge providers had not been adequate. Much of his work had been published only in the English language. Income increase due to various honours and professional rewards had accrued to him. He reasoned that his contribution towards policy and institutional reform was in a way reciprocal towards disadvantaged sections of society. He realized his conduct was not too far removed from other exploiters in society. Traders, money lenders, and other landlords extracted undue rent in the respective resource markets. Intellectuals did the same in the market of ideas.

This initiated Gupta and many of his former students and colleagues to establish the Honey Bee Network. It was evident that whatever they learnt from people must be shared with them in their own language. Hence the emphasis is on sharing findings in local languages using various media. Since the printed word would reach only literate communities, use of multimedia and multi-language technology was indispensable. Further, it was also decided that people-to-people communication can take place only when creative individuals and communities can learn in their own language. The Honey Bee newsletter is at present being brought out in six languages and an endeavour is being made to connect communities

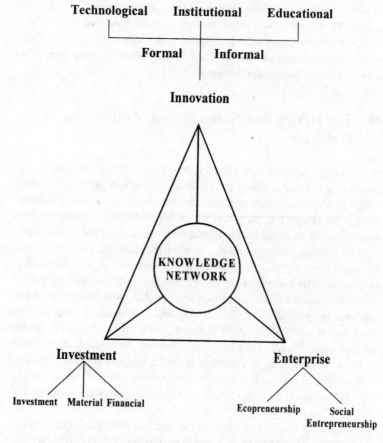

Figure 8.1   The Golden Triangle for Rewarding Creativity

around the world with each other in their own language through link language database system and communication networks. To generate mutuality, trust, reciprocity and responsibility, the Honey Bee Network decided that no individual gains will be made by use of the Honey Bee database. Thus individual consultancies are ruled out. Likewise, whatever income accrues must be shared in a reasonable manner with the providers of knowledge. Obviously, these goals and underlying principles are not easy to accomplish. The fact that the database has been growing and in many cases innovators have been seeking us out indicates that societal confidence in our philosophy is increasing. Slowly these values might become the standard practice of the profession.

A voluntary organization, SRISTI, was set up in 1993 to strengthen the Honey Bee Network in different parts of the country. SRISTI supports the Honey Bee Network by linking six E's, namely, ethics, equity, excellence, environment, education and efficiency in enterprise.

The operational framework developed to pursue the goals of the Honey Bee Network is shown in Figure 8.2 and Figure 8.3. The figures show how contemporary as well as traditional innovations are scouted, screened for experimentation for value addition or dissemination, and then rewarded through various material and non-material incentives to individuals and collectives. Policy support at macro and micro levels becomes important for conversion of innovations into products and eventually into sustainable resource use. The networking of various strategies, actors and institutions through the knowledge network leads to sustainable livelihoods apart from mechanisms for conservation of resources and knowledge around it.

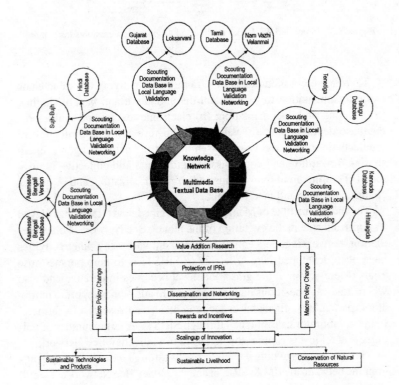

Figure 8.2 Knowledge Network Multimedia and Textual Database

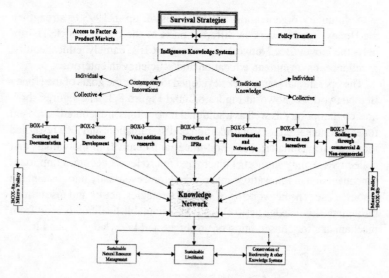

Figure 8.3 Framework for Understanding and Augmenting Grassroots Innovations

There are eight modules in this framework involving the value chain from documentation to its eventual dissemination and benefit sharing: (*a*) scouting and documentation; (*b*) electronic textual and multimedia database development; (*c*) value addition research; (*d*) protection of intellectual property rights; (*e*) dissemination and networking; (*f*) benefit sharing, rewarding and compensating individual and collective innovators; (*g*) scaling up of innovations and commercialization; and (*h*) policy changes at micro and macro levels.

The Indian Institute of Management in Ahmedabad (IIMA) has played a significant role in the evolution of the Honey Bee Network. Policy mediation, networking, conceptual development and many other activities have been developed here. The role of SRISTI is to help pursue those goals where action at the grassroots level becomes imperative and also where advocacy positions have to be taken. In addition, support to innovators, particularly, financial or technological, and research in farmers' fields or laboratories is pursued through SRISTI. A large number of volunteers at all levels support the activities of the Honey Bee Network.

Three examples of policy breakthroughs through the collaborative programme between the IIMA, SRISTI and the Honey Bee Network are worth mentioning here:

Establishment of Gujarat Grassroots Innovation Augmentation Network (GIAN): As a follow up of the International Conference on Creativity and Innovations at Grassroots organized at the IIMA in January 1997, the Gujarat government helped in setting up a fund through partnerships between civil society, state government and academic and corporate institutions. GIAN has been trying to scale up the technologies that have been utilized by the Honey Bee Network for the database maintained by SRISTI.

Presentation to the prime minister's taskforce on IT: An invited presentation on multimedia database to the taskforce was well received and a sub-group on content for IT applications drew upon this experience for developing national strategy.

Establishment of National Innovation Foundation (NIF): A presentation of multimedia databases on 26 April 1999 (to policy-makers in the ministries of finance, science and technology, departments of scientific and industrial research, agricultural research and education) and articulation of the concept in the pre-budget meeting with the finance minister led to the following announcement in the GoI budget speech:

> *Jai Vigyan* is the tribute so aptly paid by our Prime Minister to hail the achievements of our scientists. The time has come to unleash the creative potential of our scientists and innovators at grassroots level. Only then we can make India truly self-reliant and a leader in sustainable technologies. I propose a national foundation for helping innovators all over the country. This Fund, with an initial corpus of Rs 20 crore, will build a national register of innovations, mobilize intellectual property protection, set up incubators for converting innovations into viable business opportunities and help in dissemination across the country.

The NIF will try to replicate the experience of the Honey Bee Network, SRISTI and IIMA in scouting, spawning and sustaining grassroots innovations. The application of information technology will be a very vital component of NIF's strategy.

Knowledge network for sustainable technological options operationalized through the Honey Bee Network implies that innovations in one part of the world may seek or attract investments from another part, if necessary, to generate enterprises (whether commercial or noncommercial, individual or cooperative) in a third place. Several innovative experiments have been started to explore this Golden Triangle for rewarding creativity. It requires acknowledging that not all innovators may have the potential for becoming entrepreneurs or have access to investible capital. One could have an innovation say from India, an investor from Europe and an enterprise in South Africa.

■ Application of the Multimedia Database

The Honey Bee database with thousands of innovations has been upgraded to multimedia capabilities so that barriers of language, literacy and localism are overcome to connect innovators, potential entrepreneurs and investors across regions. By using electronic, textual and oral media, a multi-language node network allows individuals as well as collective grassroots innovations to be documented, experimented, disseminated and rewarded in material as well as non-material manner.

Much is said about participatory research and millions are spent in augmenting capacity of formal institutions to 'learn from people' (unfortunately using short-cut methods which are neither accountable nor ethically very sound or even scientifically very efficient). However, not even a fractional amount is spent in augmenting the capacity of innovators themselves to do research, take risks, and generate new enterprises themselves or through partnership with other entrepreneurs. Multimedia database makes it possible for innovators to become self-reliant through horizontal networks.

■ Specific Features of the Database

The database includes empirical illustrations of how small farmer men and women have developed innovative solutions to local problems through their own genius without any outside help. In addition to innovators who generate contemporary solutions, we have examples of experts who have used traditional knowledge with relevant modifications for solving problems. There is often a confusion among people to imply that: (a) all local knowledge is traditional; and (b) it is contributed and maintained by the communities. Our database shows that this is not true. There are a large number of individuals who have thought of a unique solution to either a persistent or a new problem. The need for recognizing individuals cannot be overemphasized if we want our society to become creative, meritocratic and willing to reward experimentation and innovation. There is no other way any country can become globally competitive. Further, these individuals will also act as role models to inspire the younger generation to be even more innovative.

The first screen provides entry to the database as well as a window on SRISTI. The database is in three languages, i.e., English, French and Gujarati. The French language was chosen to demonstrate global implications of the database. The first Global Knowledge Conference organized by the World Bank in 1997 was held in the French-speaking part of Canada where the database was first displayed.

The second screen introduces the viewer to various categories of innovations. In each category there are several innovators whose names and innovations are profiled. The viewer can press a button on any of these to reach the page of that innovator. The first page of every innovation (Figures 8.4 and 8.5) has a photograph of the innovator, the innovation and a brief profile of both. If there is more than one innovation, these are displayed through additional buttons. The language button is available on every page so that the viewer can switch between languages.

The most important feature of the database is that it integrates sound, picture, film and text in such a manner that even an illiterate farmer can listen to the voice and see the innovation in action to understand it. We have shown this database at several places such as the *Shodh Yatra*[4], fairs in villages and towns, informal village meetings, and in educational and policy institutions. The immediate impact of a multimedia database is that it is quicker and more apparent than textual databases.

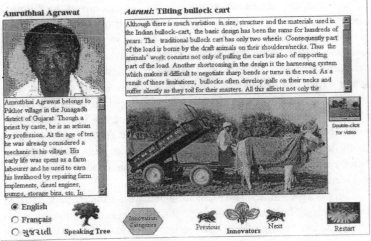

Figure 8.4 Amrutbhai Agrawat, an innovator with his innovation

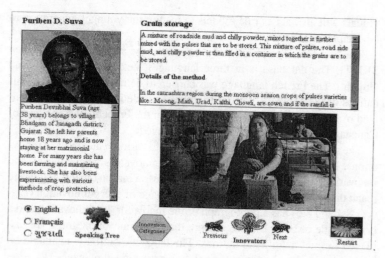

Figure 8.5   Puriben D. Suva, an innovator with her innovation

■ Other Impacts

When farmers see the faces of people like them doing extraordinary things, they certainly get inspired, as it is easier for them to identify the innovators. The impact of the innovators is even more profound in the village. The entire community seems to take pride in the fact that one of them is profiled in the database, which is seen by people in other parts of the country as well as around the world. It spurs them to bestow more recognition on their own fellow farmer innovator. On meeting tribal and other communities, the access to database often generates a question as to why a particular expert from their community is not there in the database. The demand for being scouted, catalogued and recognized helps extend the goals of Honey Bee Network immediately. Often, the innovator whose profile people watch, walks along the rest of the group in *Shodh Yatra*. This gives the people an opportunity to talk to such an innovator, and thereby demystify the technology as well as enhance the process of lateral learning.

There is a recognition and realization that innovation matters, and that too by unsung heroes and heroines. When herbal innovations are discussed, a slow but significant revaluation of the role of local knowledge experts, herbalists, etc., takes place in the local context. The same healer, who so far appeared powerless and a philanthropic do-gooder, is now seen by some as an expert worthy of respect by outsiders. Exposure to the Honey Bee database also generates a desire to experiment, particularly, when pest control or veterinary medicine innovations or outstanding traditional knowledge is discussed.

There is an observed demand of some of the local innovative products and services. This particular impact has been very significant for some innovations such as the tilting bullock cart or a simple device to fill nursery bags or an improved pulley for drawing water. The transformation of ordinary initiatives into extraordinary innovation takes place when people realize that they have lived with an inefficient or less efficient solution (for millennia as in the case of the water pulley).

The initial inertia had to be overcome among potential innovators. In some of the villages, when we showed the database to large number of people with the help of an overhead projector, we asked the farmers and artisans to share their own experiences. Occasions when there was total silence were overcome on our insisting that we would show our next card only when they will reciprocate by sharing some of their own innovations. In Hirenvil village near Gir Lion Sanctuary in Gujarat, during the night discussion, several 'unsung' heroes were discovered. One person had developed a lock system to unwind and lift a damaged submersible pump from underground—a task which is difficult and laborious. Likewise, in the village of Bhanjibhai, a person who had developed a three-wheel 10 HP tractor and a local herbalist who had developed some innovative solutions volunteered to share their experiences.

One of the unfortunate impacts has been that except in some villages, women generally sit in the rear or farther from the place where we display the database. Therefore, we have to take the notebook computer to them (Figure 8.6) so that they don't feel deprived of the exposure and, at the same time, have the opportunity to share their own creativity. In Nandapur village, district Vadodara, when the database was shown to the women they immediately identified Ataben Shantilal Bariya, an expert woman who has made remarkable grain storage bins. We must acknowledge that our database is much weaker in terms of women's innovations—something we are trying to overcome in the next phase of our action research.

■ Future Issues of Concern

We can help strengthen people-to-people learning only when we ensure communication in local languages and media. The Honey Bee Network

Figure 8.6 Display of database to women using notebook computer

has created new standards of accountability and ethics in dealing with grassroots innovations. The formal sector can not use the knowledge of the poor without acknowledgements, citation and of course prior informed consent—a notion we argued before the Convention on Biological Diversity (CBD) came into existence. Similarly, the documentation and dissemination of these innovations must take place in local languages and without exhausting IPRs of these communities and individuals. For the latter, we propose that the INSTAR system is institutionalized by the World Trade Organization (WTO) as well as CBD so that INSTAR becomes part of the knowledge network for augmenting coping strategies of the poor in a creative manner.

In a recent paper, Gupta argued that the publication of local knowledge exhausts IPRs on one hand, and on the other, may deprive the knowledge provider any benefit that may arise from value addition in local knowledge to the individual or community or nation concerned. At the same time, local language publications make it possible for people struggling with similar problems to learn from it. This happens through publication in local languages as attempted by the Honey Bee Network. However, the challenge is to marry the two goals of easy and quick opportunity for lateral learning (through local language publication), and sharing of benefits through value addition in the same knowledge.

Legitimizing databases like Honey Bee and a registration system of innovations may provide the answer. Such a registry will prevent any firm or individual to seek patent on community knowledge as well as on knowledge and innovations produced by individuals without some kind of cross-licensing. Honey Bee will then make its databases accessible to all patent offices in lieu of the protection provided to the communities and individuals whose knowledge is catalogued in it. The alternative of greater secrecy and withholding of knowledge will make every one lose through: (*a*) greater erosion of oral knowledge; (*b*) continued unwillingness of the younger generation to learn the knowledge, innovations and practices developed over a long period of time; (*c*) depriving any opportunity to knowledge holders as well as those dependent upon them to improve their livelihood prospects through sharing of possible benefits; (*d*) lack of material incentives for conservation of endangered species; (*e*) knowledge rich poor communities may migrate out due to low opportunities for subsistence and employment, and not take care of local resource or overexploit the resource itself, netting very little value in a short period of time; and (*f*) stifling the very creative and buoyant laboratory of innovations at grassroots by denying any social esteem for such knowledge through material as well as non-material incentives and general neglect.

Since it will be very difficult for any and every community to seek protection of its knowledge and inventive recipes for various purposes such as herbal pesticides, human or veterinary medicines, vegetative dyes, etc., a registration system should be developed. Such a registry will prevent any firm or individual to seek patent on community knowledge as well as on knowledge and innovations produced by individuals without some kind of cross-licensing.

Disentangling the relationship between literacy, education, knowledge and wisdom may spur education processes for young and old, if access to the database lasts longer. A suggestion is often received as to why such a database could not be based in a local school or panchayat office. The demand for decentralized access to databases on local creativity, if harnessed, can erode the inertia and charge the local imagination to try and improve things with their own efforts. The democratic, polycentric polity requires a large number of self-governed nodes, not just receiving solutions but also generating and sharing solutions. The next step in the Honey Bee multimedia database will be when local innovators would be able to not just retrieve information but also feed in their own innovations to get comments from their peers, seek intellectual property rights protection, generate demand for their services or products or even get enquiries from potential investors or entrepreneurs interested in joining hands with the innovator to scale up the innovation. Lack of education may not come in the way. In fact, the demand for education to master such technologies may increase.

■ Conclusion

The Honey Bee multimedia database has taught us a great deal about demystification of information technology and its use for empowering local communities and within them the creative women and men. We are convinced that this technology if applied properly with the right kind of sensitivity to local, cultural and ecological diversity, can transform the capacity for imagination and experimentation. A great deal of discussion on sustainable development is today top down, one way, and often based on information and alternatives produced by the formal sector. The Honey Bee database has demonstrated that by building upon the knowledge of the poor people, we can not only enrich local repertoire of ideas but also trigger initiatives some of which may transform into innovations. Whether institutional capacity to respond to these innovations will also simultaneously increase could depend upon the emergence of horizontal knowledge networks managed by local communities and individual innovators, aided by the volunteer scientists, IT experts, media planners and educationists. The Honey Bee metaphor can indeed make a difference if it can permeate our vision for promoting learning, experimentation, innovation and institutional transformation at the grassroots.

Notes

1. This paper is a modified and updated version of a paper invited by the InfoDev programme of the World Bank sponsored Global Knowledge Conference, 22–25 June 1997, Toronto, and later presented at the IIMA/World Bank workshop on Applications of ICT in Rural Development, 18–19 March 1999. The paper benefitted from the experience and inputs of several persons, including T.N. Prakash, Vivekanandan, S. Sharma, P. Geervani, Murali Krishna and other volunteers who generously shared their insights and innovations including Srinivas Chokkakula, Neeraj Joshi, Riya Sinha, Samir, Chandrani, Pawan Mehra, Dileep Koradia, Rajesh Patel, Unnikrishnan, Hema Patel, Vidyulata and Amit Pandya. The volunteer team was lead by Prof. Brij Kothari. The database is in three languages—Gujarati, English and French—to facilitate people-to-people communication and learning. The French translation was facilitated by Alliance Française.

2. Such roads increase the reach of loggers and also reduce their transaction costs (all at

public expenses) while local tribal communities are exploited because an indifferent state fails to protect their property rights as well as livelihood options. Land alienation takes place rapidly despite laws to the contrary in existence and highly skilled tribal communities (skill of dealing with nature) are converted into the pool of 'unskilled labour'. Road and other infrastructure do not empower these local communities in the same proportion as it does their exploiters.

3. http://csf.coloardo.edu/sristi/
4. Journey on foot through forests, tribal villages and other rural areas to scout local innovators, honour the already scouted knowledge experts at their home, and encourage dialogue among travelling conservators, innovators and local communities.

References

Bhatnagar, S.C., 1992, Use of Information Technology in Rural Development: Lessons from the Indian Experiences, in S.C. Bhatnagar and Gumthar Cyranek (eds), *Technology Transfer for Development: The Prospects and Limitation of IT*, Tata McGraw-Hill, New Delhi, pp. 31–43.

————, 1995, Application of IT in Grameen Bank, in Mayuri Odedra-Straub (ed.), *IT and Socio Economic Development*, Ivy League Publication, USA.

Bhatnagar, S.C., Rama Rao, T.P., and **Bhat, Chetan,** 1991, Computerization of Land Records, Computer and Remote Sensing Applications in Rural Development, February.

Kaul, Mohan, 1979a, Framework for Organising District Information Service Centres, Indian Institute of Management, Ahmedabad, Working Paper No 238.

————, 1979b, Implementation of Information Processing Systems, Indian Institute of Management, Ahmedabad, Working Paper No 283.

————, 1980, Monitoring and Evaluation System for Rural Development in India, in Kuldeep Mathur and Inayatullah (eds), *Monitoring and Evaluation of Rural Development: Some Asian Experiences*. Asian and Pacific Development Administration Centre, Kualalumpur, Malaysia.

Patel, Nitin R., and **Madhavan, T.,** 1977, Utility Theory and Participation in Unfair Lotteries, Indian Institute of Management, Ahmedabad, Working Paper No.186.

————, 1984, Planning for Rural Roads in India, Indian Institute of Management, Ahmedabad, Working Paper No 494.

9

A Wired Village: The Warana Experiment

N. VIJAYADITYA

The primary objective of the 'wired village' project is to demonstrate the effective use of IT infrastructure in the accelerated socio-economic development of villages around Warana Nagar in the Kolhapur and Sangli districts of the state of Maharashtra. This paper describes the activities involved in setting up the wired village and the applications that have been implemented.

■ Introduction

Ushering in the information technology (IT) revolution to villages where more than 70 per cent of the Indian population lives is a dream that has come true at Warana in the Kolhapur district of Maharashtra. The special IT taskforce set up by the prime minister recommended modernizing the cooperative movement through use of state-of-the-art information technology. This led to the 'wired village' project initiated by the Prime Minister's Office (PMO).

The key objective of the project is to demonstrate the effective contribution of an ICT infrastructure to the socio-economic development of a cluster of 70 contiguous villages around Warana Nagar in the Kolhapur and Sangli districts of Maharashtra.

The project aims to:

- Utilize IT to increase the efficiency and productivity of the existing cooperative enterprise by setting up a state-of-the-art computer communications network;
- provide agricultural, medical and educational information to villagers at facilitation booths in their villages;
- provide communication facilities at the booths to link villages to the Warana Cooperative complex;
- bring the world's knowledge at the doorstep of villagers through the Internet via the National Informatics Centre Network (NICNET);

- provide distance education to both primary and higher educational institutes; and
- establish a Geographic Information System (GIS) of the surrounding 70 villages leading to greater transparency in administration especially in matters related to land.

■ Project Partners and Costs

The Warana Project is jointly carried out by the National Informatics Centre (NIC) (on behalf of the central government), the Government of Maharashtra and the Warana *Vibhag Shikshan Mandal* (WVSM) (education department). The estimated cost of the project is around $600,000 (Rs 2.6 crores). Of the total cost of the project, 50 per cent is being borne by the central government, 40 per cent by the Government of Maharashtra and the remaining 10 per cent by the WVSM.

■ The Project Area

Warana Nagar, situated on the banks of the Warana river, lies in a green valley about 35 km (21.86 miles) from the city of Kolhapur, and about 400 km (250 miles) from Mumbai. The transformation of Wararna from a barren to its current prosperous and fertile region began with the setting-up of a cooperative sugar factory near the village of Kodoli in 1959.

The Warana Cooperative Complex was a forerunner of integrated rural development involving the cooperative movement that has had a classic ingredient of success—peoples' participation. The Warana cooperative sugar factory initiated this movement that has resulted in the formation of over 25 cooperative societies related to sugar, milk and poultry production. The total annual turnover of these societies exceeds $1.5 million (Rs 6.5 crores approx.). Most of the societies are located within a radius of 4 km (2.5 miles). The complex has its own EPABX facility for voice communication between various centres and societies. Some of the societies such as sugar and dairy have computerized their routine operations.

The sugar factory is the backbone of the Warana complex. 'Weaker' sections of society have experienced economic growth and a level of prosperity unimagined earlier as a result of direct employment. The sugar factory has won several awards for its efficiency and productivity. The Warana paper mill was set up to utilize the waste products of the sugar factory. A distillery has also been set up in the complex. An electricity generation unit has been set up using the waste water of the paper mill and the distillery. The energy generated by the unit is used by the paper mill.

The Warana complex is designed to look after all the basic needs of the workers. They have been provided with living quarters, filtered water, inexpensive electricity, schools, physical training and cultural centres.

The Sugar Administrative Building (SAB)

The sugar administrative building, situated in the heart of Warana Nagar, houses the administrative staff of the sugar, distillery and paper factories. The sugar factory is located around 500 metres from this building. The sugarcane for the factory is obtained from roughly 70 villages located in the districts of Kolhapur and Sangli.

Warana Cooperative Milk Producing Society—Dairy

The factory for processing milk-related products is situated approximately 3km (1.86 miles) from the sugar administrative building. This office of the dairy has stand-alone computers for its data processing. (Some of the important milk products include pasteurized milk, milk powder, ghee, butter and *sreekhand*—a sweet dish made of curd (yoghurt) and sugar. Approximately 2 metric tonnes of *sreekhand* is sold in Mumbai daily). The factory processes about 200,000 litres of milk per day collected from the surrounding 176 villages in the districts of Sangli, Satara and Kolhapur. Factory management has shown a keen interest in computerization and networking, and to complement these tasks, has emphasized training of staff.

Warana Grahak Mandal (Warana Bazaar)

This is the largest bazaar in Warana with an annual turnover of $7.3 million (Rs 31.4 crores approx.). It has two department stores in Warana Nagar and Wadgaon in addition to 29 retail outlets in 78 villages spread across Kolhapur and Sangli. Managing the flow of goods like bazaar purchases directly from various factories requires a reliable communications network to book the orders and follow up through e-mail. Daily statistics from each of these retail outlets is also required by the management.

Goods Processing Society (WAGPCOS)

This society has been set up for processing agricultural goods in packaged form. The raw material for this is obtained from a large number of villages in various districts. The machinery has been imported and the installation is nearing completion.

Mahatma Gandhi Medical Trust

This modern, 200-bed hospital equipped with state-of-the-art technology is located 10 km (6.25 miles) from the sugar administrative building.

Warana Cooperative Bank

The main branch of the bank is a two-storeyed building located about 1 km (0.6 mile) from the main sugar administrative building. It has 20 branches in Kolhapur and Sangli districts. Most of these are within a 30 km (18.75 miles) radius from the main branch. The annual turnover of this bank is nearly $7 million (Rs 30 crores).

Warana Vibhag Shikshan Mandal

The college is spread across 500 sq. m at a distance of around 750 m from the administrative building. It houses the engineering college, polytechnic and the college of arts and science. The engineering college offers courses in mechanical, chemical, civil and electronics engineering. A course in computer science will be offered starting in the academic year 1999–2000. The engineering college has over 1,000 students. The colleges have ample space for the installation of VSAT that can be utilized by a large number of users of the institute. The engineering college has about 100 Pentium and 486 based computers out of which about 50 systems are connected by LAN. The college authorities plan to have a campus-wide fibre-optic LAN to facilitate faster communication to be paid for with their own funds.

■ Project Responsibilities

To make sure that the work is carried out smoothly the responsibilities of various departments have been identified. The responsibilities of NIC are to: (*a*) supply the hardware, networking sub-systems and associated software; (*b*) design, supply and establish the communication infrastructure with Internet access; (*c*) install and configure an Intranet; (*d*) provide site preparation guidelines; (*e*) design, develop and implement the application software; and (*f*) provide training on application software.

The responsibilities of the Government of Maharashtra are to: (*a*) barcode product/items at Warana bazaar; (*b*) design and prepare MIN card with hologram and bar-code for a villager's database; and (*c*) purchase the GIS.

The responsibilities of the WVSM are to: (*a*) provide sites and site preparation; (*b*) provide 10 telephone lines at sugar administrative building, and one at each IT centre and facilitation booth; (*c*) enter and validate all data; (*d*) recruit technical manpower for managing the centres; and (*e*) provide necessary infrastructure support to the staff of NIC on tour to the sites.

■ Project Implementation

Two committees have been established to oversee implementation of the project, a project coordination committee and a project implementation committee. The project coordination committee has responsibility of planning, designing and coordinating implementation of the project. The project implementation committee looks after day-to-day tasks and ensures speedy implementation. The project coordination committee, after detailed discussions with the villagers, the staff at the engineering college, government officials and other Warana officials, prepared the implementation plan.

These two committees met at regular intervals during project preparation to follow up the work progress, technology, and to review and reallocate resources. The committees invited experts in communication technology, government administration and academics to ensure quality and to reach the best possible solution in the proposed environment.

■ Wired Warana – The Infrastructure

With a view to provide complete connectivity to the 70 villages in the Warana region, a three-tier structure was implemented. The sugar administrative building and the engineering college form the main hub centre, the first tier. The business centres (6) and IT centres (6) are at the next level while the facilitation booths (70) provide connectivity down to the village level.

The sugar administrative building was selected as the hub for business centres. Facilitation booths have access to the building and business centres through a dial-up network. To provide a rugged and reliable network, a high-speed wireless LAN is provided at the business centres. The VSAT and Mast for omni-directional antenna of the wireless LAN has been installed on the sugar administrative building. A high speed IPA VSAT is connected to a hub for Internet access. A 30-foot Mast on the roof of the building has been constructed for installation of an omni-directional antenna for a wireless LAN with a bandwidth of 2 Mbps. The radio modem of the wireless LAN is connected to the hub. The wireless LAN technology has been used to provide reliable Intranet/Internet connectivity to the busines centres. All existing machines are integrated in a LAN environment with two additional NT servers and four windows-95 clients. A proxy server is also installed which acts as a firewall.

The engineering college was chosen as the hub for the Intranet accessed by all village booths. A high speed IPA VSAT is installed, connected to a hub. The Warana web-server is installed at the college. It hosts the web-based applications. A bank of 10 dial-up lines with modems is interfaced through a router to provide SLIP/PPP connectivity. All existing machines are integrated in the LAN environment, and a proxy server is installed which acts as a firewall to the Internet. The same server also functions as an e-mail server. E-mail accounts are created in this server for all users at the facilitation booths, IT and business centres.

The business centre sites includes the dairy, Warana bazaar, WAGPCOS, Mahatma Gandhi Hospital, and the Warana Cooperative Bank. The business centres access the wireless LAN via a unidirectional antenna installed on the rooftop of each of the centres. A wireless LAN is set up at the centres which can communicate with the central VSAT installed on the sugar administrative office. The bank is also connected to the networks through a unidirectional antenna located on the roof of the main branch.

Six villages at a distance of nearly 10 km (6.25 miles) from Warana Nagar have been identified as sites for the IT centres. The idea is to provide IT facilities as close to the villages as possible. The computers are set up in a room 20 ft × 20 ft in size.

The centres provide facilities for distance education, computer-assisted instruction, and access to Indira Gandhi National Open University (IGNOU). Each IT centre has a LAN environment using structured cabling, with a 'receive only' VSAT (DirecPC) and a dial-up link. The operating system on the computers is Windows-95, and HTML browser is installed for accessing the web-server. Currently six villages have IT centres: Mangale, Pargaon, Dhole, Nagaon, Satwe and Kodoli.

Facilitation booths are being set up in 70 villages (more than 30 booths are currently operational). They have a dial-up facility to link to the central hub located at the sugar administrative building. Each booth has a Windows-95 multimedia computer equipped with a modem (33.6 Kbps) for the dial-up link. It is configured for SLIP/PPP. The computer has multimedia facility, a handheld scanner, a bar-code reader and a 132-column printer. An HTML browser is installed for web access. Eudora e-mail is configured for SMTP mail service.

■ The Software Applications

From the requirements analysis carried out by NIC, 15 applications were identified for implementation. These can be grouped as web-based and network-based applications.

Web-based applications: Six applications can be accessed by villagers from the facilitation booths. They provide information about employment and agricultural schemes, information on government procedures, automated assistance in completing applications for government certificates such as ration cards and birth and death certificates, crop information, information on bus and railway services, medical facilities, and water supply details. From the booth the villager can interact with the Warana management to register grievances and seek redressal. Agricultural marketing information is available from the Warana web-server giving market arrival and daily rates of various regulated commodities. It is possible for students to seek guidance from the booths by accessing educational and vocational information.

Other applications: The sugar factory is actively involved with farmers in cultivation, cutting, testing and transportation of the crop. These activities ensure an information exchange between the factory and farmers, which are manpower intensive. A management information system for sugarcane cultivation developed by NIC leads to speedy and accurate data exchange between the factory and the farmers using the village facilitation booths. The land records application permits villagers to view and print extracts using data from a land database stored on a compact disc, or from the *tehasil*[1] site right at their village booth. Dairy is the mainstay of the Warana Complex. The computerization of dairy activities will permit milk collection and analysis to be made available to villagers at the booth as soon as it is generated.

The Warana bazaar (Warana *Grahak Mandal*) is a cooperative with the largest departmental store in Warana. The maintenance of this inventory is a major activity. A bar-code-based computerized inventory system is being developed for the bazaar.

A Geographical Information System (GIS) has also been developed. It includes a base map of the neighbouring 70 villages, socio-economic information such as schools, population, land under cultivation and linking cadestral maps and 7/12 extracts in Marathi (the regional language of Maharashtra) to the GIS.

The IT centres have been set up with a view to provide computer-based education facilities to the village children. AUTNIC, a computer-based self-learning and testing aid, is provided at the IT centres to support the course curriculum. The WVSM plans to prepare a multiple-choice question bank for all school grades for each subject using AUTNIC. This question bank will help the students gain insight into their course-ware with a better understanding of the concepts covered.

■ Implementation

In order to comply with the time schedule of six months and establish the basic network, NIC deployed professionals from various fields. Twenty engineers put in over a man–month each in Warana, to ensure functioning of the sites at the business and IT centres, the village facilitation booths, and the overall network.

Over 50 software professionals have been involved full-time in application development since June 1998. Each team handling an application has been interacting regularly with their Warana counterparts, visiting the Warana site, discussing and finalizing the specifications, the implementation strategy and delivering as per the approved strategy signed and agreed upon by NIC, GoM and WVSM. On the basis of specifications drawn up with end users, prototypes of the applications have been built, demonstrated at the user sites and further modifications made. All the applications have been installed at Warana, after approval and acceptance by the users.

The software developed for Warana is the single largest set of applications developed in the client-server/web-based environment in Marathi.

The software has been delivered complete with detailed operational manuals in Marathi for the local Warana users.

■ Human Resource Development

Extensive training on the applications and administration of the network has been provided to Warana users on site as well as at Pune. Selected teaching staff of the engineering college are trained to manage the network.

The training aims at creating an awareness in the villagers regarding the utility and benefits of state-of-the-art equipment made available at Warana. It has also provided the required skill level to the operators to handle the machines and assist the villagers. The operating level staff at the hub centres have been given sufficient training on site as well as at NIC to confidently manage the network.

This project has proved helpful in generating employment opportunities for the local population. The facilitation booths in each of the 70 villages will employ an operator each, and the five business centres will have two qualified computer experts each to manage web and e-mail administration, Windows-NT and database administration. Apart from this, each of the six IT centres will employ two skilled computer operators. Fifteen operators have already been recruited for the IT centres and village booths to assist users in using e-mail, data transfer, and other applications.

The Warana Project is the forerunner to many such rural development projects envisaged by the IT taskforce. It would enable villagers to access sources of both local and global knowledge, and help provide transparency in administration.

Notes

1. A *tehasil* is a unit of administration above the village and below a sub-division.

10

Inmarsat Experience in Village Telephony

RAJ GUPTA

Recognizing the commercial and social benefits of telecommunications, an increasing number of governments have declared provisioning of telecom access in rural and remote areas as a social service obligation of telecom operators in their respective countries. In fact, provisioning of telecom access in far-flung villages and other remote areas is expensive to install and maintain, and the traffic volume is low. Telecom operators are, therefore, looking for newer technologies which are cost-effective for use in such areas. Inmarsat large antenna mini-m systems provide cost-effective means of providing global telecom access in areas which are far removed from terrestrial switching centres and where traffic is expected to be low. Inmarsat, in cooperation with Indian Department of Telecommunications (DoT), carried out a pilot project to demonstrate this system. The system has been found to be technically and commercially viable for such areas. The telephone systems in the pilot sites have been used by the villagers to derive commercial benefits besides making personal calls.

■ Introduction

The linkage between tele-densities and national gross domestic product (GDP) has been recognized worldwide. The International Telecommunications Union (ITU) has estimated that 1 per cent investment in telecommunications results in 3 per cent increase in GDP. ITU studies of tele-densities in developing countries show that these low tele-densities are deceptive as the majority (70 per cent–80 per cent) of the total telephones are located in urban areas having a population of only 20 per cent–30 per cent, while the remaining 70 per cent–80 per cent of population shares 20 per cent–30 per cent of telephones.

An increasing number of countries are recognizing the benefits of provision of telecom access in rural and remote areas as a part of universal service obligations. The Government of India made universal service obligation one of the main objectives of the 1994 National Telecom Policy. There are about 607,000 villages in India of which 300,000 are yet to be provided with telecom accessibility. The government, through policy announcements and through the draft of the new telecom policy, has reiterated its priority to cover the remaining villages in the Ninth Five Year Plan (1997–2002).

Provision of telecom access to rural and remote areas is expensive, of low usage, and geographically difficult. It is, therefore, required that telecom operators judiciously select a technology that is cost-effective and easy to maintain.

■ Technology Used

For the selection of appropriate technology, the factors to be considered are geographical location, its remoteness from the switching centre, anticipated traffic volume, and capital and operating costs. The technology options available are terrestrial lines/cables, MARR (Multi-access Rural Radio), WLL (Wireless Local Loop) and satellite. Villages that are closer to the switching centres can easily be covered by terrestrial and cellular systems; the places which are located between 5 and 25 km (3.13 and 15.66 miles) from the switching centre can be covered by microwave systems such as MARR and WLL, while places located beyond 25 km (15.63 miles) from the nearest switching centres and those in hilly areas can best be covered through satellite-based systems.

	Population Million	%	No of DELs '000	DEL %	DEL Per 100 Persons
Rural	627.1	74.2	530	10.5	0.08
Urban	217.1	25.7	4545	89.5	2.1

Source: 1991 Census

Figure 10.1   Distribution of Telephones between Urban and Rural Areas

■ Inmarsat Large Antenna Mini-M System

The International Mobile Satellite Organization (INMARSAT) has been providing highly reliable communication services worldwide for over two decades. Its Large Antenna Mini-M (LAMM) system is suitable for providing communications in rural and remote areas. To demonstrate the technical and commercial viability of this service in the provisioning of village public telephones (VPT) in rural and remote areas, the Department of Telecommunications, Videsh Sanchar Nigam Limited and the Inmarsat jointly conducted a pilot project, under a MoU signed in April 1997. Under the pilot project, 13 VPTs were installed in a wide geographic variety of village sites throughout India, including hilly areas of Jammu and Kashmir, the deserts of Rajasthan, remote villages in Uttar Pradesh, and in coastal areas of Maharashtra and Andhra Pradesh.

The choice of technology, between LAMM and Very Small Aperture Terminal (VSAT), was based on the expected traffic volume. The Inmarsat LAMM system is the ideal choice, where the volume is expected to be less than 20 minutes per day.

While the Inmarsat LAMM is positioned for slow and fast speed of deployment and low and medium bandwidth requirement, VSATs are normally suitable for slow speed–high bandwidth requirements.

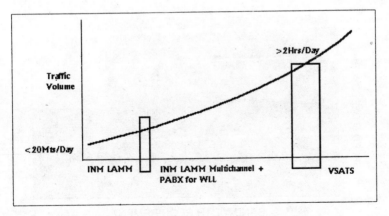

Source: VILCOM Satellite Communications & Traffic Management Services

Figure 10.2   Inmarsat LAMM and VSATs

There are considerable differences in equipment and installation costs for Inmarsat LAMM, VSAT TDMA (Time Division Multiple Access) and VSAT SCPC (Satellite Personal Communication System). The equipment and installation cost of the Inmarsat LAMM is noticeably the lowest while that of VSAT SCPC is the highest.

In terms of functionality, satellite-based communication systems with handheld terminals, popularly known as the Global Mobile Personal Communications System is best suited for voice communication. Inmarsat LAMM system is the best choice for both voice and low speed data transfer. And VSAT-based system is best for large-scale data transfer.

The VPT consists of an Inmarsat Mini-M terminal, a large dish antenna for high gain (–7dBk), 50 × 50 × 1 cm, a VPT monitor with a printer and an optional solar power supply.

The pilot project successfully established the technical feasibility and cost-effectiveness in the provisioning of village public call office (PCOs) in remote, hilly and geographically difficult areas. The sites selected for the pilot project were a fair representation of varying environmental and physical conditions such as high altitude, deserts and coastal areas that reflect the rural hinterland of India.

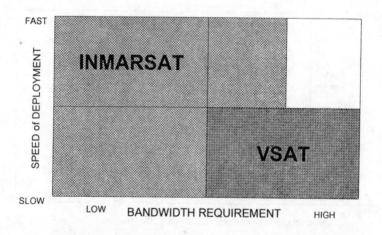

Figure 10.3 Competitive Positioning Deployment & Data Capability

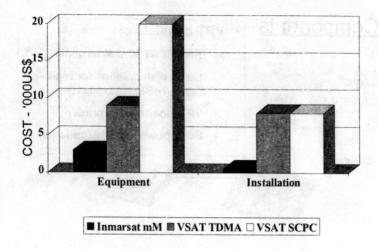

Figure 10.4   Estimated Equipment & Installation Cost

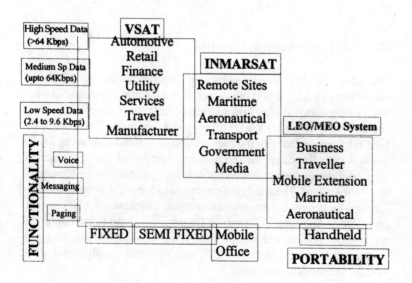

Figure 10.5   Functionality–Portability

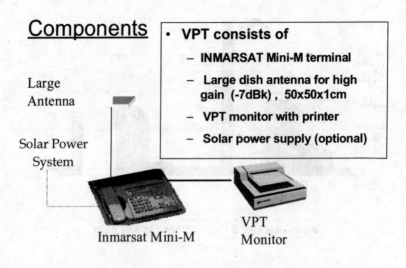

Components

- **VPT consists of**
  - **INMARSAT Mini-M terminal**
  - **Large dish antenna for high gain (-7dBk), 50x50x1cm**
  - **VPT monitor with printer**
  - **Solar power supply (optional)**

Large Antenna

Solar Power System

Inmarsat Mini-M

VPT Monitor

Figure 10.6   Rural Village Public Telephone(VPT)

■ Implementation Results

The set-up was found to be technically suitable for providing telecom access in rural, remote and hilly areas, using LAMM terminals. The terminals were set up in a few hours and franchisees (unskilled) were able to operate the system after a brief training of a few hours. The system has been fully integrated with the Indian telecom network, including DoT's tariffs that are based on the distance and duration of the call. Users of these satellite phones are thus charged on the same basis as the terrestrial-based subscribers. The whole set-up is transparent as far as users are concerned. The system has minimum power and maintenance requirements, and exhibits high availability (over 98 per cent). Simple operation and maintenance provide a high degree of system reliability. While the pilots were up and running, the solar, UPS and VPT call monitoring devices were all successfully integrated.

Commercially, the pilot project demonstrated satisfactory, average, daily utilization, a high degree of customer satisfaction, and frequent use of the facility.

■ Distribution of Calls

Analysis of calls from the pilot project supplemented by studies conducted by independent institutions suggested that 40 per cent of the total calls made were for personal reasons, 30 per cent were official, 20 per cent were business, and 10 per cent were miscellaneous.

■ Benefits of Telephone Facilities

To users: The benefits of the use of telephone facilities can be broadly categorized as personal and commercial. On the personal front, the phones enabled villagers to keep in touch with their relatives and friends. Commercially, villagers used the telephone to obtain information on the prices of their agricultural inputs and for marketing their products. This enabled them to reduce the cost of their inputs and increase the value of their produce by comparing the prices in nearby *mandis* (markets). Farmers now covered by VPTs are not only aware of the price of inputs but also about the latest innovations of technology such as high-yielding varieties, optimum use of insecticides, pesticides and fertilizers, which have enabled them to get better yield. In becoming commercially more vigilant, villagers have reduced their dependence on exploitative middlemen. A socio-economic 'bonus' has been to create job opportunities in the rural areas related to using the VPTs.

To the government: As for the government, the telephone facilities can be seen to have both tangible and intangible benefits, including reduction of human migration from rural to urban areas and the public's travelling time and costs. The government may consider providing healthcare and education through tele-medicine and tele-education facilities, and using the system to improve law and order. The VPTs have proven to be of immense help in disaster relief and rescue operations, as well as in typical situations such as religious processions and elections.

■ Financing PCOs

PCOs could be financed through budgetary allocation by government out of the licence fee from the Basic and Cellular Services, by financial institutions such as the Asian Development Bank and the World Bank or through part financing by government and telecom operators. The operating costs could be covered by collection from users of domestic calls (which have been made affordable) and international calls (for which premium service is to be charged at higher rates to partly cross-subsidize domestic calls). Cross-subsidization could also be done by telecom operators from other services. The government could also directly subsidize the operating costs over a limited period of time.

■ Conclusion

Inmarsat LAMM service is a low cost, easily maintainable, quickly implementable solution for providing highly reliable satellite-based communication in rural and remote areas. This technology is being increasingly used or planned to be used in many developed and developing countries. Countries that have used or are planning to use this technology include Australia, Nigeria, Morocco, Sudan, Brazil, China and India. This technology provides a very cost-effective solution for meeting the objective of universal service obligation in rural and remote areas. However, to keep tariffs low, and to keep the services commercially viable, the system needs some help and support in the initial years from respective governments, telecom operators and financial institutions.

PART V

Use of ICT for Training in Rural Areas

11

Satcom for Extension Training

B.S. BHATIA

As far back as 1975, the development and educational communication unit at the Indian Space Research Organization (ISRO) has been involved in experiments where the humble television and the hi-tech satellite were combined to provide broadcast education and information to districts throughout India. Now the benefits of technological advances in communication technology are being deployed for extension training at the block level. This paper describes applications of the satellite network, opportunities and constraints in rural development. It also presents results of a recent project in Jhabua, a predominantly tribal district in Madhya Pradesh.

■ Introduction

India has been committed to the use of science and technology to meet the challenges of national development. Speaking at the UN Conference on the Peaceful Uses of Outer Space, Dr Vikram Sarabhai, the founder of the Indian space programme said, 'there are some who question the relevance of space activities in developing nations. To us there is no ambiguity of purpose. We do not have the fantasy of competing with the economically advanced nations in the exploration of the moon or the planets, or manned space flights. But we are convinced that if we are to play a meaningful role nationally and in the community of nations, we must be second to none in the application of advanced technologies to the real problems of man and society which we find in our country.' Thus the genesis of the Indian space programme was based on potential applications of space technology in dealing with the problems of a developing society.

An important task in the process of development is that of carrying information on the latest agriculture, health, and other areas of concern to rural areas. For this purpose, India started agricultural extension services in the early 1950s. Today extension agencies exist from the state capital to the district, block, and village levels in all areas of development such as agriculture, health, family planning, social welfare (including women and children), and education. Besides these extension services there is a chain of elected representatives at state, district, block and village levels who facilitate extension work. With the introduction of *panchayati raj*[1] these institutions are expected to play a vital role in the process of development. Each state, therefore, employs a few hundred thousand extension workers and has a similar number of elected representatives, who have to be trained and regularly updated with information related to development.

The conventional method of training and information dissemination through the extension channel has been based on a cascade model: master trainers are trained; they in turn train the trainers who go to the field for conducting training of extension workers; extension agents carry information to the final recipients. This model has obvious disadvantages such as loss of information, degradation of quality of training, long lead times and high costs. In fact, the lead time of such a training cycle is so long that by the time one training cycle is completed, the second is overdue. There is therefore a great need to expedite the extension process and enhance its quality. It is in this area that satellite communication can be of critical importance.

Satellite communications technology (Satcom) offers the unique capability of being able to simultaneously reach out to large numbers spread over large distances even in the remotest corners of the country. It is a very strong tool to support development education. Satcom has been used both in a broadcast mode as well as in an interactive mode to reach out to rural audiences at large, and to conduct training programmes for extension staff as well as rural population who are participating in the implementation of development activities.

■ Satellite Broadcasting

India was amongst the first countries to explore the use of Satcom to support development and today its space efforts are recognized the world over for their wide spectrum of applications relevant to societal benefit. The efforts started in the mid-1960s when it undertook the first major experiment to use Satcom for developmental communication, namely, the Satellite Instructional Television Experiment (SITE) in 1975–76. Under this project direct reception sets (DRS) were installed in 2,400 villages spread over six states, and four hours of rural development oriented programmes were transmitted every day. A primary school teachers' training programme was organized during summer vacations. A number of studies were conducted to evaluate the impact of SITE. Some major observations of these studies are as follows:

- It is possible to deploy, operate and maintain community TV sets and DRS even in remote areas of a country, reaching out to 80–90 per cent of the rural population.
- Community viewing is possible, and an average audience size of 80–100 can be expected in each centre.
- Instructional programmes were preferred to entertainment programmes.
- Substantial gains were possible in the areas of health, hygiene and nutrition. The most dramatic gains were registered by illiterate viewers.
- Despite case studies of innovations adopted in agriculture as a result of TV programmes, a large-scale survey did not show any statistically significant gains.
- Community access to TV tends to narrow the communications-effect gap.

A primary school teachers' training programme was conducted as part of SITE, in which 40,000 teachers were trained at 2,400 receive sites. The evaluation of this training indicated that a statistically significant gain was found in content of science knowledge of the trainees as a result of multimedia package training. Most of the teachers felt that the training was useful. They also found that TV, rather than radio, was preferred for the training.

Overall, SITE established that the extension of communications infrastructure to remote areas is not only feasible, but that it can contribute tremendously to promote development/extension education and training.

The broadcast systems have several limitations when used for educational and development purposes. These include wastage and the difficulty of coordinating ground support efforts with the broadcast. Besides, broadcasting systems do not provide for any interaction between the resource person and the learner, which is essential in both educational and training situations. To overcome these limitations, India has been experimenting with the use of one-way video and two-way audio teleconferencing interactive networks for education and training. This has been found to be of immense use and has been made operational in the form of Training and Development Communication Channel (TDCC) (see Figure 11.1).

■ Training and Development Communication Channel

Configuration

The network consists of three major elements: the teaching end, the spacecraft and the classroom. The teaching end consists of a small studio and an 'uplink' earth station. It originates the training material either in the form of 'live' lectures or recorded video programmes from a small studio and uplinks these television signals to a geostationary communication satellite (INSAT-2C) by means of an uplink earth station located at the teaching end. One extended C-band transponder on INSAT-2C has been earmarked for this purpose. The classroom has a DRS/Rx-terminal capable of receiving a signal in extended C-band from the satellite. The talkback is possible through normal STD telephone and fax connection provided in the classroom. In case a location does not have an STD connection, a satellite talkback terminal can be used. The question from the classroom is received at the studio and fed to the system so that it is heard live over the network to all viewers. The resource person at the teaching end provides the answer/feedback. The system thus provides a one-way video and two-way audio teleconferencing network, supported by a fax machine.

Applications

Three major applications of this network have emerged: distance education, rural development and industrial training.

In the field of distance education, a number of user agencies offer diploma and degree programmes in a distance education mode to students all over the country. The Indira Gandhi National Open University (IGNOU) is a leading institution in the field of distance education. Several states have set up state level open universities. Several professional agencies such as the All India Management Association (AIMA), and the Institution of Electronics and Telecommunications (IETE) are offering diploma programmes to students. These agencies have found the use of such a network most effective in reaching out to students as well as counsellors.

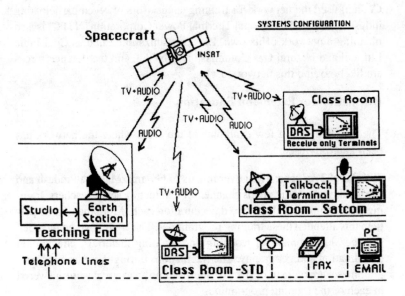

Figure 11.1 Training and Development Communication Channel

These agencies have installed their own receive terminals for regular use of the network.

In the area of rural development, the network is finding application in the training of extension staff of various departments of the state governments. The network has been used by the governments of Gujarat, Madhya Pradesh, Karnataka and Goa for training watershed management and health extension officials. Training of rural women under the Development of Women and Children in Rural Areas (DWACRA) programme has been carried out. Important areas in which the network has been used include training of *panchayati raj* elected representatives, primary school teachers and Integrated Child Development Scheme (ICDS) workers. These are the areas in which very large numbers spread over large distances have to be trained. Only a network such as this overcomes the disadvantages of distance and numbers.

In industrial training the network has been used by large multi-locational organizations like the State Bank of India (SBI) for training participants all over the country. The SBI has set up a network with 46 classrooms, has conducted two training programmes and plans to conduct more. It also plans to start its own network. The National Productivity

Council used the network for training supervisors of seven participating industrial units. The National Thermal Power Corporation (NTPC) is also planning a network of its own. Large organizations such as Coal India Ltd, Oil and Natural Gas Commission (ONGC), and the defence forces are likely to find this network useful.

Utilization for Extension Education

The following are a few examples of the areas where the network has been gainfully used.

Teachers' Training: The governments of Gujarat, Madhya Pradesh and Karnataka have utilized this channel for conducting seven teachers' training programmes of about two days duration each. More than 6,900 participants attended these training programmes. The areas covered included science, development of teaching and learning materials, educational coordination and geography. The interactions during these training programmes were quite intensive; 10 questions on an average were answered in each of the training programmes.

Tests to evaluate the effectiveness of the Special Orientation Programmes for Teachers (SOPT) revealed the following (Phalachandra 1997):

- 82 per cent of the participants found this method better than the traditional method of training.
- Achievement tests indicated significant gain in knowledge in five out of the nine topics covered.
- Answers given by experts were found to be satisfactory, relevant, and useful.
- The teachers found that the programme was 'effective', 'created interest', increased their 'enthusiasm' and 'improved [their] capabilities'.
- The participants and facilitators participated with enthusiasm, took an active part in the activities and adapted themselves easily to the new training technique (teleconferencing).
- Listening to the questions and answers of fellow colleagues of other centres was a worthwhile experience for most participants.
- Participants found the programme more interactive, interesting and effective as compared to the traditional mode. They suggested the extension of this technology-based training programme to other areas such as language teaching and mathematics.

The experiment demonstrated the effective use of one-way video and two-way audio technology as an alternative mode of training. The teleconferencing mode was found to be feasible to orient/train individuals spread over a vast geographical area. Each team had master trainers to avoid transmission loss.

Almost all state governments have utilized the network for reaching out to the elected representatives of the *panchayati raj*. The Karnataka state government conducted a special programme for women representatives, Madhya Pradesh for the members of the block (*janpad*) panchayats, and Gujarat conducted a series of programmes on the *Gokul Gram Yojana*.[2] The Goa government conducted a 10-day training programme for its panchayat members. The major topics related to the effective functioning of the panchayats, conduct of *gram sabhas* and roles, responsibilities and powers of *gram* panchayats.[3]

The response in all the cases was overwhelming. In the three-day training programme of Madhya Pradesh, more than 1,800 representatives participated, and about 100 questions were received on telephone and 2,000 on fax. In Goa for a 10-day programme, attendance varied between 45 and 150 per receive centre with 10 to 25 questions per session.

ICDS Workers' Training: The department of women and child development organized several training programmes for ICDS workers in Madhya Pradesh because in this state there are some 120,000 ICDS workers' assistants. It has now been realized that the only way to reach out to these numbers is by setting up a network at the block level and organizing regular training programmes every month.

The network has been utilized for training and extension education in every area of development, including health, agriculture and watershed management. Several user agencies and state governments have installed receiver networks. There are 500 terminals in the network and this is being expanded to 1,500. State governments are making investments to set up their own studios and uplinks. During 1998, 97 training programmes were organized for over 186 days, and more than 1,000 participants were trained in each programme. With the network becoming digital, it will be possible to operate several channels simultaneously.

Major Advantages of the System

- Training, in the shortest period of time, a large number of geographically dispersed people;

- multiplier effect by trainers;
- uniformity of the training content;
- access to the best available learning resources, irrespective of the geographical location of the learners;
- repeatability of training courses/educational packages;
- enhanced involvement of the trainers/learners due to interaction, leading to greater learning gains;
- system capable of allowing different user groups to share the network. Specific topics for specific locations and specific groups are also possible; and
- significant cuts in expenditure due to savings in travel, logistics and replication of teaching infrastructure.

■ Jhabua Development Communications Project (JDCP)

This is a project undertaken in Jhabua, a predominantly tribal district of Madhya Pradesh, adjoining the western border of Gujarat. This project combines the features of satellite broadcasting as well as interactive training at the district level (see Figure 11.2).

Under this project, 150 direct reception TV sets were installed in the villages and 12 satellite-based interactive talkback terminals were installed at block headquarters. Every evening for two hours, development-oriented programmes are broadcast over the network and the interactive terminal for training. This evening telecast provides communication support to developmental activities such as health, education, watershed management, agriculture, forestry, and *panchayati raj*. The interactive training programmes cater to the training needs of a variety of block and village level functionaries, such as teachers, *aanganwadi* workers,[4] joint forest management committees, and *panchayati 'karmis'*.[5]

This system, operational since November 1996, has been evaluated and studied carefully. The research was divided into three phases: formative, process, and summative. A large-scale survey, with experimental and control villages and data collected during the project, was conducted to determine the programme's impact. The analysis indicates that:

- Community viewing has reached about 35 per cent of the rural population of which 17 per cent were regular viewers.
- Average attendance per set per day was approximately 40 persons.

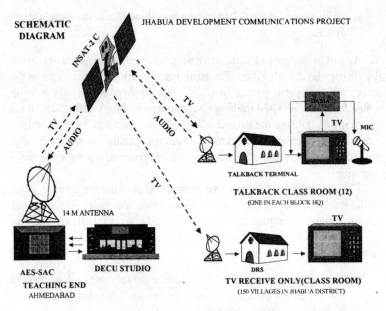

Figure 11.2 Overview of the Jhabua Development Communications Project

- The percentage of regular male viewers was more than double that of female viewers.
- There was a significant increase in the percentage (53 per cent to 74 per cent) of viewers discussing the JDCP programmes after viewing them.
- About three-fourths of the viewers enjoyed watching the programmes and found them informative.
- About one-sixth of the viewers did not follow the programmes. The T_2 survey indicated that about a half of them (7.3 per cent) did not understand the language or the topic.
- In the T_1 survey, only one-fourth of the respondents mentioned 'farm improvement' and the percentages of those mentioning 'increased awareness' in different areas varied from 0.5 per cent (*panchayati raj*) to 9 per cent (health). But in the T_2 survey, 37 per cent mentioned 'farm improvement', and the percentages of those mentioning 'increased awareness' in different areas rose from 20 per cent (*panchayati raj*) to 28 per cent (health).
- The intake of alcohol apparently decreased due to the education

programmes. About 20 per cent mentioned 'less drinking' due to JDCP.

As part of this project, interactive training programmes were organized by district-level authorities. The participants were expected to go to the block office to participate. District officials prepared a quarterly training calendar and conducted training programmes for block and village-level participants. During the project about 100 programmes were organized covering joint forestry management, education, health, women's self-help, agriculture, and watershed management. Most programmes were of a day's duration.

The experience of interactive training at the district level is quite different from that at the state level as described under Training and Development Communications Channel (TDCC). Organizing training programmes with district-level resources is more difficult than at the state level due to the following reasons:

- The information supplied by resource persons at the district level and the seriousness of the resource persons is inadequate.
- Field-level organization and logistic support is weak.
- Organizers run out of topics for training, and thus tend to become repetitive.
- Participants complain that no new information is imparted, and that only the tasks related to specific development schemes are repeated.
- Participation level decreases, because of poor organization and in-adequate quality of training.

Observations

The experience of utilizing the network for extension education and training over a long period, spread over different areas, has indicated the following:

- The system enables one to reach out to large numbers in an interactive mode. On an average, each 'receive' location has about 45 participants though the number varies, and there have been situations with much larger numbers. But from a learning and interaction point of view, large numbers is not advisable. With an average of 45 participants and 20 terminals, the number of participants in a training programme is about 900. With networks being extended to the block level, the number of participants may increase.

- Interactivity over the network is high. Participants ask more questions than time allows to be answered. In a one-hour session, at least half an hour should be provided for questions.
- Resource persons come better prepared when participating on the network since his work gets importance, is acknowledged by larger numbers and the situation is more challenging. This improves the quality of training.
- The seriousness of the training programme increases, as the coverage becomes larger, and the level of resource persons and participation of dignitaries also increases.
- The system provides a direct access to senior officials and decision makers who would otherwise be beyond the reach of participants. This gives them an opportunity to present their problems directly to high authorities.
- Participants find this communication method interesting and effective. Learning is equivalent to face-to-face interaction.
- Technology is not a barrier for participants. Even illiterate persons adapt to the learning and communication environment within a few minutes.
- Logistics and organizational aspects need greater attention. Advance preparation is required to ensure participants reach the distant locations, background material is distributed, and boarding and lodging are well managed.
- The system is most effectively utilized at the state level, because at the district level the quality of resource persons is not satisfactory and officials tend to take it as an additional work burden. Logistic arrangements are found to be better for state-level training programmes.
- It remains to be seen how the system functions when the number of classrooms increase from 20 to 200. This will be a major change and the functioning of the system will need to be reviewed.

An important issue is who in the state should operate the system. It has to be operated as a facility that several departments should be able to utilize for their training. One possibility is that it is operated by the State Institute of Rural Development (SIRD). Most extension training is related to rural development, and SIRD, which is co-located in most states with the Academy of Administration or the State Training Institute, could be an important organization to operate the system. The possibility of creating an autonomous, self-financing agency, to operate this facility should be explored.

■ Future Plans

The experience of utilizing the network has convinced state governments of its efficacy in extension education. Hence the existing networks are being extended to the block levels, and state governments are setting up their own 'Teaching-ends' including studios and uplink facilities. Mechanisms for operations and continuous utilization of the network are being defined.

For optimal use of satellite capacity, it is essential to ensure that digital technology is utilized. The networks will be converted to digital. This will enable simultaneous operation of four channels in place of one (using the same satellite capacity). This will also enable the addition of features such as two-way video from select centres and data broadcasting.

Efforts are underway to create such networks in almost all states, so that this becomes a backbone for extension training throughout India. However, this would imply a major change in the extension training methods of state government agencies. They will have to be oriented to the effective use of the medium.

Notes

1. System wherein five members of the village are elected and made responsible for its smooth functioning.
2. A village development scheme started by the chief minister of Gujarat. It aims at creating minimal infrastructure and facilities in each village.
3. *Gram* or village panchayat is the elected body of five senior members of the village, responsible for the effective functioning of the village.
4. The government has established *aanganwadi* (or creche) in each village where small children of working parents can be looked after. A village girl from each village is appointed to look after the children. She is refered to as *aanganwadi* worker.
5. People who work according to directions of the village panchayat.

References

Phalachandra, B., 1997, Report on Primary Teachers Training through Interactive Video Technology—Tele-SOPT Programme. Department of Teacher Education and Extension, NCERT, New Delhi.

12

Satcom for Barefoot Women Managers

REEMA NANAVATY

The Self Employed Women's Association (SEWA) is a trade union representing poor, self-employed women workers. SEWA's main goals are to organize women workers to be fully employed and self-reliant. SEWA has recently been using the satellite talkback communication system to conduct educational programmes that cut across a range of capacity building themes: organizing; leadership building; forestry; water conservation; health education; child development; *panchayati raj* system; and financial services. Using the satcom facility, SEWA's community groups and organizations have quick and easy communication with block- and district-level functionaries. This enables experience sharing and enriches knowledge bases.

■ Introduction

SEWA was established in 1972. It has a membership of around 212,000 women spread over 790 villages in nine districts of Gujarat. Most of the areas where SEWA works are drought-prone desert areas, where there is lack of employment, low wages, poor health, low literacy, crushing debts and high rates of forced migration, especially among men.

From 20 years of experience we have learned some hard lessons: most important, the basis of obtaining higher wages is a capacity and power to bargain. However, workers become weak and vulnerable by lack of employment. In a situation where there is almost unending supply of labour and limited employment opportunities, workers are unable to bargain for higher wages.

SEWA supports its members to organize into groups or cooperatives, so that the self-employed women themselves become owners and managers of the programmes. SEWA's approach has been to initiate programmes based on demand, organize the women, facilitate building the member's own local organization, which then takes over the programme implementation, expansion and future planning. The second major lesson is that the sustainability and self-reliance of any programme and local organization depends on its managers. SEWA works to build capacities of local managers.

SEWA has conducted training in nine districts throughout Gujarat. However, it has only one training team and its subjects are the same. Therefore, it takes time to reach members. Many demands are not met. SEWA has recently started using satellite communications in order to meet this demand for training. The network consists of three major elements—the teaching end; the receiving end; and the spacecraft—as described in the section on Training and Development Communication Channel (TDCC) in the previous chapter.

■ Methodology

SEWA's training attempts to transfer professional knowledge to the grass-roots level to increase the competencies of its members to function with alternative models.

In order to have maximum usage and impact of this medium, SEWA first conducted a half-day orientation programme. The focus was on the following:

- What is satellite communication and how does it work?
- How to design a training programme?
- Selection and orientation of resource persons.
- Role of district centre coordinator during the programme.
- Use of question–answer session.
- Feedback and evaluation.

SEWA plans to institutionalize the satcom training programme to build its cadre of 'barefoot managers'. Our satcom training programmes, each two days long, have been conducted by SEWA on the following subjects:

- Organizing training for capacity building;
- women and *panchayati raj*;[1]
- women and forestry;
- women and water; and
- savings and women.

■ Review of Training Programmes

Organization building: The aim of the training was to educate participants to organize and to identify leadership qualities and understand the roles and responsibilities of a leader. Participants included rural members and local women leaders of SEWA from the districts. About 115 women from nine centres participated in the talkback programme. The classroom training used different types of issues as ice-breakers, such as how to build a fort to bring out the importance of collective strength and the role of a leader.

Women and *panchayati raj*: In villages, panchayats have turned into training grounds for women who had been excluded from a role in village politics for millenia. The aim of the programme was to share with elected panchayat members their experiences as heads of the panchayat or members of the panchayat. The *panchayati raj* structure was also explained. This was designed to increase the awareness level of women panchayat members and facilitate their playing an ever-growing role in the panchayat. The participants included the *sarpanch* (head of the panchayat), members, *taluka* (a sub-unit of the district of which there are about 50,000 in India*)* panchayat members and delegates. About 170 panchayat members participated.[2]

Women and forestry: The aim of the programme is to highlight the key roles women play in eco-regeneration. It focused on how forestry directly affects the livelihoods of rural communities, and the potential leadership role women play in regenerating forests. About 405 members participated in the talkback programme from 12 districts.

Women and water: SEWA's input to the state's campaign is to increase women's awareness about their problems and their possible solutions, and highlight their capacity to address, solve and monitor problems by cooperating with government officials, village leaders and other village members. This particular programme had technical difficulties and had to be discontinued after the first day.

■ Lessons and Experience

The satcom talkback programmes were effective in reaching a large number of SEWA groups in rural communities, within a limited period of time. Thus the organization's outreach capacity for awareness raising, sharing experience and learning increased rapidly. An average of 150 questions or experiences were shared, and some common issues came out that cut across sectors, for instance:

- When will the government announcement to appoint woman *talati*[3] be implemented?
- In the absence of electric supply, how can farmers cultivate?
- What can be done if primary teachers are not knowledgeable or trained?
- What if a new *sarpanch* changes the previous panchayat resolutions?
- Who should be contacted to design sewerage schemes for the village?

The resource persons involved in the training summarized their conclusions as follows:

- Interactive training is useful to reach a large number of beneficiaries, and is appropriate for extension activities.
- The satcom is useful for mobilizing and conducting campaigns.
- Rural women benefit by becoming familiar with modern technology they can use.
- 'Barefoot managers' can be trained through this medium in a variety of subjects.

■ Constraints

SEWA is currently using receiving centres and infrastructure of the local government at the district level. Often, due to lack of communication and coordination, many receiving centres do not function well. There are problems of non-reception due to a lack of technical know-how at the district level. Certain operational difficulties, such as power failure, interrupt transmission.

Participation is also constrained due to the lack of talkback time or busy telecommunication lines. Hence, the centres have to either keep the telephone lines open or keep trying for longer time periods.

■ The Future

After testing this communication medium, SEWA plans to continue using it for education and capacity building, particularly, to build a cadre of local leaders and managers. The following programmes are expected to be delivered:

- Organizing skill development;
- minimum wages for different trades and its campaign;
- home-based workers' recognition and campaign;
- women and water-related programmes;
- women and forestry;
- women and health education;
- child development and nutrition; and
- capacity building of 'barefoot (local, rural) managers' through interactive sessions focusing on strategic planning, management and programme administration.

■ Conclusion

SEWA serves largely hand-to-mouth hardworking self-employed women—those making incense sticks, doing some construction job, stitching clothes on her sewing machine at home, or selling vegetables on the streets. It is an institution of totally downtrodden women, which is now trying to expand its reach through modern ICT. Distance classroom training has now been tried and usefully demonstrated as a communications tool to train women leading the programmes, helping them and the programmes to become self-reliant.

Notes

1. Nearly a million women in India have been elected to these village governing councils since India adopted a constitutional amendment in 1993 that set aside a third of all panchayat seats and village chiefs' positions for women.
2. Like men, women panchayat leaders are involved in obtaining village land for schools, selecting families who will qualify for government housing and deciding how to distribute brick lanes, latrines, electricity, etc.
3. Secretary of the village panchayat (government employee).

13

Effective Use of Information and Communication Technology for Physically and Socially Disadvantaged Groups

BHUSHAN PUNANI

Realizing the significance of information technology for persons with disabilities, the Blind People's Association (BPA) of Gujarat has made an all-out attempt to computerize its internal operations and to set up a computer-based training centre. This paper examines the tools used at the BPA for the blind and visually impaired, and analyzes constraints to diffuse this technology to other similar organizations. Some good examples are provided of individuals who have benefited from the availability of training in information technology.

■ Introduction

In India, the opportunities for persons with disabilities (PWD) as compared to their population are negligible. Paradoxically, these meagre opportunities are largely confined to the cities while 83 per cent of the disabled population resides in rural areas. Most organizations dedicated to PWD deal in skill training, counselling, vocational training, placement and to a certain extent parental training. Although, progress has been made in these human resource development programmes, the facilities provided to PWDs remain pathetically low.

Lack of coordination and an absence of networking amongst different centres and organizations are the factors most responsible for the restricted growth of programmes, inferior quality of services, inappropriate vocational training, and the fact that these reviews have not spread to rural areas. These organizations prefer the conventional approach of providing residential accommodation and imparting training in traditional crafts.

■ Need for Adopting Information Technology

The potential of information technology needs to be exploited for the socio-economic rehabilitation of physically disadvantaged groups. The major benefits assured by adopting this technology are highlighted:

New avenues of employment: Information technology is emerging as the single largest avenue for both formal as well as self-employment. If provided appropriate training and right exposure to computer literacy and use of IT, the disabled could also compete with their normal counterparts.

Range of services: The PWD must be provided multi-dimensional services that start with assessment of the individual, functional and vocational training, and mobilization of resources for their development. It is difficult for any single organization to provide the complete gamut of such services. The most practical and viable option would be to develop coordination using modern information and communication technologies, like in the western countries where rehabilitation centres offer comprehensive services utilizing new technologies. The incorporation of ICT will be of tremendous use for programme development, service delivery, access to and dissemination of information.

During the early 1980s, the Blind People's Association (BPA) of Gujarat, in its endeavours to adopt IT, made a number of efforts aimed at introducing technology into the organization, which included developing a system of monthly reports in a standard format. It gradually evolved to develop computer software for analysis of reports, reimbursement of expenses and compilation of statistical information. BPA used various software for analysis of data for research and began to use multimedia to train PWD. For this it procured PCs, LAN system, printers and an Internet connection.

Special equipment for enabling blind persons to access computers through auditory means was later installed. Along with this, the BPA imported a special computer and a reading machine. Software to enable persons with lower visibility to read print material was also installed.

In 1994, the department of employment and training, Government of Gujarat recognized the BPA's computer training and telephone operating courses under the Industrial Training Institute (ITI) stream. This is for the first time in the country that an ITI exclusively for persons with disabilities has been granted recognition by the State Council for Vocational Training. Efforts are now being made to seek recognition from the National Council for Vocational Training. The training centre at BPA has trained 120 PWD. This centre also conducts refresher courses.

■ Special Equipment

To facilitate the use of IT by the blind, the BPA imported and installed the following equipment.

Speech synthesizer: This enables a blind person to read text in both the DOS and Windows environment. An operator can access the computer in three ways:

- For the synthesizer to speak what one types into the computer;
- to access information on the screen when one is in 'live' mode, thus one can communicate directly with the computer through the keyboard; and
- in some cases, the output on the screen is also spoken.

However, this equipment has its limitations as graphics or fancy text cannot be read from the screen.

Braille printer:[1] This can be attached to the computer. It produces double-sided interpoint braille at 100 characters per second on a single sheet of paper. It has an internal speech system that speaks out all set-up parameters. A multi-copy facility enables the user to produce up to 99 copies of a document, again releasing the computer for other work while printing continues. Whenever required, the operator can print the screen and verify the current sequence of commands.

Braille translator: This software converts English text into braille saving hours of tedious manual labour (Shah 1999).

The Reading Edge: This is the first completely integrated reading machine for the blind and the visually impaired. It combines an advanced speech synthesizer, intelligent character recognition, and a bookedge scanner into one lightweight, portable machine. It works like a photocopying machine; the difference is that instead of printing, it reads aloud. When one scans a page, it converts the image of the page into data. The software analyzes the image data and converts the same into text. It automatically saves all the scanned text in its memory thus enabling blind and visually impaired persons to read the English text independently.

Visibility—low vision reading software: Visibility is a software programme that converts a PC compatible computer and a scanner into an intelligent magnification and reading system. It magnifies text on the screen display making it possible for low vision persons to read.

■ Limiting Factors

Despite the immense potential of this technology, its diffusion in India has remained confined to a few centres, due to the following reasons:

Non-availability of indigenous technology: The major limiting factor is the non-availability of technology. All the special equipment has to be procured from abroad.

Limited training facilities: Only a few centres have been established in the country for imparting training to visually impaired persons in the use of this equipment.

Language barrier: Most of the equipment available is in English or in other foreign languages, while school education in India is mainly in Hindi or in regional languages.

Expensive technology: This technology is expensive and beyond the financial capacity of most users in India.

Unsuccessful attempts: The government has established the Science and Technology Mission (S&T Mission) for persons with disabilities. This mission had sponsored some projects to develop a speech synthesizer, a braille embosser, a close circuit television and a talking computer. But, unfortunately, no equipment has reached its prospective consumers. Ironically, by the time the speech synthesizer was developed, the technology was already obsolete. Moreover, no back-up support services were provided. As a result, the equipment remained confined to the shelves of the research institute.

■ Case Studies

Undoubtedly, there is large scope for adapting and using ICT for enhancing functional capacity and improving the employment potential of disabled people. To establish this fact, a few persons who have benefited immensely from the use of this technology were contacted and their achievements have been briefly described.

Akbarkhan

Akbarkhan, born blind, completed his graduation and did a course in stenography before he joined the Punjab National Bank as a stenographer. Being ambitious, Akbar had the zeal to move on. On learning that the Blind People's Association has started a computer training course for the blind, he approached the bank authorities and got their permission to join it. On reaching Ahmedabad, he pursued this course in computer operation in DOS as well as Windows environment with the help of a speech synthesizer. He recorded his lessons using a cassette player, prepared notes using a braille printer and read the English text by using the Reading Edge.

With the help of innovations and adaptations in information technology, within six months, Akbar learnt programming in Dbase, the operation of WordStar, and the use of DOS commands. He will now be learning programming in other languages and the operation of MS Office-97. Akbar will become the first blind computer programmer with Punjab National Bank. Winner of the National Award as the Most Outstanding Employee for the year 1989, he is likely to be promoted as programming officer, which would be a landmark achievement for all blind people in the country.

Sipai Jakir

As a small boy of 5, Jakir was paralyzed from the waist down because of polio. Despite odds, he passed his Class X examination from special schools, where he was one of the many disabled children. After joining a regular school, he realized that the disabled were either mocked or pitied. To overcome this handicap, Jakir joined a computer programming course at the BPA.

He learnt to use the computer and started his professional career with part-time consultancy jobs in computer companies and was finally employed by the BPA for its in-house software development. Today, Jakir is independent and is supporting his family of six. His most outstanding achievement is that now he is training visually impaired persons in the use of special devices, to enable them to operate computers and do programming. He intends to take up software development and advanced graphics as a career.

Ghanshyam M. Limbachia

Ghanshyam M. Limbachia was born without legs. He completed his Bachelor's Degree in commerce with flying colours. He then decided to try his luck in the field of computers. So he joined the Cama Computer Centre run by the BPA, where he soon became a programmer.

Beginning his life from scratch, today Ghanshyam earns more than $240 (Rs 10,300 approx.) a month, which is a fairly decent income. He is working as an instructor in a computer consultancy firm and is also a freelance computer consultant. He is now a well-known software consultant for a number of units at the Gujarat Industries Development Corporation, Kalol, as well as other industrial plants in Ahmedabad.

Yahya Hakimudin Sapatwala

Yahya, because of a family genetic incongruence, was born with optic atrophy. Fighting his destiny Yahya completed his schooling in the BPA School where his education, boarding and lodging were free. After this he specialized in Gujarati literature at St Xavier's College. He stood first in the university and won a Gold Medal. He then proceeded to do his Master's Degree in Gujarati from Mumbai University, and obtained a Gold Medal in this course too. He also did Bachelor's in Education (B.Ed.). He could successfully operate a computer but found it difficult to access the print material. With the help of the Reading Edge, he was able to access the print material. Because of this facility, he has prepared lectures on 'Administration of Special Schools' for teachers of blind institutions. He has joined, in June 1999, one of the reputed public schools in Ahmedabad as a teacher.

These are just a few examples. Hundreds of visually impaired persons have benefited immensely from recent advances in information technology. Information technology has the potential of granting a new lease of life to millions of less-privileged people.

■ Need for Investment to Promote ICT

In India, there are about 300 schools for the blind providing special education to about 18,000 visually impaired children. Besides these, there are a large number of integrated education programmes imparting education to about 12,000 children. However, there are hardly any facilities for imparting training in the use of special equipment and computer-aided devices. This is because to establish an IT centre to enable students to learn the use of speech synthesizers, braille embossers, Talking Edge and other screen reading software requires an exorbitant investment of about $24,000 (Rs 10.3 lakhs). If at least the most important organizations have such facilities they would be in a position to impart training to 400 visually impaired persons every year. For a country which has a population of almost 4,000,000 visually impaired persons, imparting training to only 400 selected persons may not be a significant breakthrough, but would certainly be a good start. According to available estimates, imparting training to all 30,000 visually impaired students studying under different modes of education, over a period of five years, would require an investment of about $360,000 (Rs 154 lakhs). Considering the lack of resources of the government, it is desirable to establish at least 20 such training centres in the country.

■ Futuristic Approach

All over the world efforts are being made to encourage the use of information technology for enhancing functional capabilities, performance, employability, competitiveness and mainstreaming of PWD (ESCAP 1999; Ramani 1999). The principal objective of these innovative approaches is to enable these disabled people to access information independently. For this the main requirements would be to provide them with access to the following:

DAISY consortium: Digital Audio-based Information System (DAISY) is a worldwide coalition of libraries and institutions (Kerscher and Kjele 1998). The digitization of books provides opportunities to increase the quality and availability of information. The consortium will be of international standards developed by the International Standards Organization (ISO), World Wide Web Consortium (W3C), Hyper Text Markup Language (HTML) and Extensible Markup Language (XML).

Talking software: A large number of visually impaired people across the world are using a variety of talking and screen reading software for operating computers in Windows. This user-friendly, versatile software costs as much as a Pentium-II computer.

Tools for braille power: A large number of companies have developed a variety of braille embossers. These have the capacity of embossing text, signs and graphics on paper, metal or plastic sheet.

Braille translation software: Braille provides a reading medium for blind people, using 'cells' made up of raised dots in various patterns instead of the characters used in regular print. A braille translation software provides translation and formatting facilities to automate the process of conversion from regular print to braille (and vice versa). It also provides word processing facilities for working directly in braille as well as in print. A unique braille transaction software which enables the user to produce material in *Bharati* (Indian) braille has been developed. One of its unique features is that one can produce *Bharati* braille in regional languages using the English keyboard. It is also easy to learn, and allows a number of copies.

The Economic and Social Commission for Asia (ESCAP) is investigating setting up Community Tele-service Centres (CTCs). The CTC would be a multipurpose communication-based facility designed to provide multiple services for improvement of rural telecommunications, rural healthcare and education, broadcasting of meteorological information, disaster monitoring and relief, natural resource management, protection of environment and development planning (Bayarsuren et al. 1999; Libreso 1999).

The ESCAP Working Group in Satellite Communications, recently decided to extend the benefits of CTCs to socially disadvantaged groups. It recommended that satellite communication technology be used to help PWD network and mutually support themselves by fostering awareness of the value of indigenous knowledge and skills. This could be an important use of ICT for the rehabilitation of socially and physically disadvantaged groups in the ESCAP region.

Notes

1. Braille is a six dot system of embossing that substitutes for characters used in regular print, providing a reading medium for the blind.

References

Bayarsuren, G. et al., 1999, Mobile Community Teleservice Centre System: Applications for Nomadic Countries. A paper presented to the ESCAP Regional Working Group on Satellite Communication Applications, Tehran, March.

ESCAP Report, 1999, Work of the Regional Working Group on Satellite Communication Applications, Tehran, March.

Kerscher, George and **Kjele, Hansson**, 1998, DAISY Consortium—Developing the Next Generation of Digital Talking Books, *Web Post*, February.

Libreso, Felex, 1999, Operationalizing the Community Tele-service Center (CTC) Concept: A Pilot Model for the Philippines. Paper presented at the Fourth Meeting of the Regional Working Group on Satellite Communication Applications, Tehran, March.

Ramani, R., 1999, Satellite Communication Applications for Rural Development. Paper presented at the Fourth Meeting of the Regional Working Group on Satellite Communication Applications, Tehran, March.

Shah, Vileen, 1999, Usha Braille Translation Software. Chicago: Braille America, Mimeograph.

14

Same Language Subtitling for Literacy: Small Change for Colossal Gains

BRIJ KOTHARI AND JOE TAKEDA[1]

Same Language Subtitling (SLS) refers to the idea of subtitling motion media programmes in the same language and script associated with the audio track. This apparently small change in certain popular cultural programming contexts on television and cinema, especially, film songs, has shown enormous promise for literacy skill improvement among neo-literate and in generating interest for literacy on a national scale. Overwhelming support for the technique has been found in several field tests in Gujarat, involving both literate and neo-literate people. A controlled experiment with school children has demonstrated that SLS leads to improved reading because it whets people's interest to sing along and know the lyrics. The effectiveness of SLS lies in the improvement of reading skills—a subliminal by-product of widely popular entertainment.

The SLS approach can be implemented easily in several regional languages. As compared to the enormous amount of money spent by the National Literacy Mission (NLM) and state-level agencies on post-literacy with poor returns on investment, the resource commitment involved in SLS is ridiculously low and the potential gains, phenomenally high. Yet, the idea has caught the imagination of few national-level policy-makers in media and education. While the main focus of the study was on SLS for film-song programmes on television, implementing SLS in a CD-ROM and television context with songs of social change was further explored.

■ Introduction

If the masses of people in India are to benefit from the dizzy pace of developments in information and communication technologies (ICTs), the country requires a good infrastructure, both in terms of 'hard' and 'soft' dimensions. For instance, let us consider one of the most promising ICT—the Internet. Just as telecommunications is the 'hard' infrastructure necessary for the Internet revolution, literacy is a critical aspect of the 'soft' infrastructure that will fundamentally determine the extent and nature of such a revolution. At the turn of the millennium, even if the telecommunications infrastructure in India were to enjoy total coverage at high bandwidths, the worldwide Internet would hardly be able to include in its web a small fraction of India's population due to literacy and language barriers. Only half of the adults in the country are literate.

Speculatively, only half of the literate may be literate enough to be able to take advantage of text-based matter in books or on the Internet. Another major impediment is that English predominates on the web. Even two of the most spoken languages in the world, namely, Hindi and Bengali, can hardly claim a trifling byte of the cyber world. Thus, if there is to be a widespread information revolution in India, the top priority has to be universal literacy, at levels that are adequately high to enable direct benefits to people. Simultaneously, information riding on ICTs would need to be in vernaculars. This chapter is about using television, an increasingly ubiquitous communication technology in India, for the development of a 'soft' infrastructure for the ICT revolution.

■ Same Language Subtitling (SLS)

SLS refers to the verbatim replication of audio and text in the same language. From the viewers' perspective, the text they see and the sound they hear reinforce each other in perfect synchronization. For instance, in SLS the audio track in Gujarati would find its reflection in Gujarati text on the screen—no translation, no transliteration, simply, word for word copy of audio and text. Subtitling has almost always been trapped in a translation mindset or used for providing additional information. Subtitling in the same language is, to a certain extent, counter-intuitive. It is at times used by advertisers to reinforce their message but is rarely employed in regular media programming.

The SLS technique has been implemented in two different communication technology contexts to subtitle songs. The aim is to create an environment for the subliminal improvement of literacy skills in everyday media interaction and in educational situations. SLS has been found to contribute to the development of literacy skills in experimental settings. The experiments underscore the potential contribution that the SLS concept could make towards national literacy development in a lifelong or continuing education sense. A sustained effort has already been made to concretize the idea by implementation in film-based songs. The second method to use SLS for literacy is in 'stills in sync', in songs of social change. The idea has been implemented in technology but field tests have not yet been carried out.

While the efforts of the National Literacy Mission (NLM) have made a noteworthy contribution in increasing the number of neo-literate[2] through the Total Literacy Campaign (TLC) mode (Athreya and Chunkath 1996) its post-literacy and continuing education initiatives have not been able to address the very serious problems of skill erosion and relapse. Many of the literate in India relapse into illiteracy due to lack of practice opportunities in everyday life. The evaluation Report of the Expert Group (1994), commissioned by the NLM itself, made several important observations: (*a*) fragility of literacy achievements leading to relapse is as serious a problem as the lack of widespread literacy; relapse could be as high as 40 per cent; (*b*) women constitute two-thirds to three-fourths of the adult neo-literate resulting from TLCs; and (*c*) the problems of illiteracy, and by extension, relapse, are most acute in the Hindi heartland. The report adds further, 'literacy will have to be connected to everyday existence in very concrete and sustainable ways'. Learning contexts would have to make a transition from 'guided learning to self-reliant learning'. The use of SLS can be rationalized on the basis of these observations.

Indian television has witnessed a virtual explosion of film- and pop song-based programmes in vernaculars, especially in Hindi, to an extent that some channels are exclusively dedicated to such programmes. Moreover, song-based programmes are known to attract high, across the board, viewership especially among female viewers (Sinha and Parmar 1995). With the simple and inexpensive addition of SLS to these programmes, one could achieve substantial literacy skill gains over a passage of time among the neo-literate masses in the country. SLS of popular song programmes on television successfully creates an entertaining environment for literacy skill-based transactions. The power of SLS is not in creating 'educational' programmes, but in enhancing the entertainment of the existing programmes. Literacy skill development is a subconscious by-product.

Audience Feedback

The potential and practicality of implementing SLS was underlined by the results of eight field tests conducted to gauge audience reaction in rural and urban Gujarat (Kothari 1998). The results confirm that audiences overwhelmingly preferred subtitled over unsubtitled song programmes. Several reasons were offered for this preference. A majority of the people liked the idea of being able to sing along with the help of the displayed song lyrics, and being able to follow the words better due to the complementary influence of audio and text on each other. Children, especially, evinced a tendency to overtly sing along with the help of the subtitles. The subtitling method did not prove a hindrance in terms of interference with the picture.

Controlled Experiment

A controlled and sustained experiment to evaluate the contribution of SLS towards reading skill improvement is underway for the last three months in a Gujarati-medium municipal school in Ahmedabad. The Hindi film songs recorded from *Chitrahaar*[3] were subtitled. They were then shown three times a week to children in Grade IV, who do not have a formal education in Hindi, and to the ones in Grade V, who are taught Hindi in school. The three experimental groups are: A—five subtitled Hindi film songs shown in each session; B—same five Hindi film songs, but unsubtitled, shown in each session; and C—control group, sees nothing. A session comprised five songs to mimic *Chitrahaar*. The same pre- and post-test was used to measure reading ability of unconnected words. The test comprised 38 mono-syllable words and 20 two, three, and four syllable words each. The mono-syllable words were created to cover nearly all the sounds and *matras* (roughly translated as vowels) existing in Hindi. Words having two to four syllables were taken randomly from the songs shown. Children's reading of the words was recorded and simultaneously marked for mistakes—syllable-wise—on a separate sheet. After 35 viewing sessions a post-test was conducted (see Figure 14.1).

The analysis revealed an improvement on an individual's syllable as well as on the entire word level. Table 14.1 shows the average number of syllable-level improvement for mono to four syllable words in groups A (with subtitle), B (without subtitle) and C (control group).

In a short span of three months, it was evident that SLS of film songs does contribute to reading improvement. The observations revealed that the subtitled group's improvement over the unsubtitled group is noticeable in mono, two and three syllable words, and not as much in four

Table 14.1 Average syllable-level reading improvement for different word lengths

Treatment	Mono-syllable	Two syllables	Three syllables	Four syllables
A: With subtitle	1.05	2.70	3.90	4.30
B: Without subtitle	0.26	1.00	2.50	4.05
C: Control group	−1.15	0.42	2.28	1.44
N=20 for each group				

Figure 14.1 Children watching Same Language Subtitling film songs[4]

syllable words. Both the subtitled and unsubtitled groups did better than the control group, suggesting that merely watching song programmes repeatedly contributes to familiarity with language and is reflected in improved reading skills.

Another measure of the effect of SLS is the improvement in the average number of words read perfectly (as shown in Table 14.2). This measure conveys the 'step' improvements and is different from the incremental syllable-level improvements of Table 14.1.

Table 14.2   Average word-level reading improvement for different word lengths

Treatment	Two syllables	Three syllables	Four syllables
A: With subtitle	1.60	1.10	0.90
B: Without subtitle	0.23	1.14	1.23
C: Control group	0.47	0.44	−0.44
N=20 for each group			

The average improvement at the entire word level was most apparent for two syllable words, for the group that viewed the subtitled programmes. For three and four syllable words, the group difference was marginal. Both the treatment groups did better than the control group, again supporting the pattern noticed in Table 14.1.

Children in the subtitled groups were more inclined to sing. Of the 35 sessions, 25 were monitored for overt reading/singing along. Individuals in the subtitled group were observed to sing along an average of 3.5 of the 25 sessions. In the unsubtitled group, the same figure for self-induced and overt reading/singing was 1.89. Singing along occurred on its own in a context in which it was not suggested through the programme or by the facilitators. In a live broadcast setting, this innate urge to sing along can be actively encouraged by the person anchoring the programme.

■ Potential and Prospects

Both the audience reaction and a sustained viewing of these programmes by children have strengthened the case for implementing SLS in a broadcast setting. This simple addition to existing film-song programmes shown on television was found to enhance entertainment for the literate and the neo-literate. The enhanced entertainment has been demonstrated to invite singing along and/or reading, thus, creating greater interactivity between the television and the viewer. Ultimately, this everyday practice is expected to improve literacy skill levels as a subconscious process.

Though improvement of reading skill has been argued to occur through SLS, another likely outcome is the creation of a reading culture. When a neo-literate (or non-literate) sees another neo-literate or literate reading and singing along with popular songs, he/she is motivated to do the same. In the Indian rural context, where one witnesses relatively fewer reading/

writing transactions, an increasing number of people are transacting with television, primarily to derive entertainment. SLS uses the reach and attraction for film-song programmes on television to create a more entertaining environment in which reading transactions can be integrated.

In all the Indian languages that have a thriving film industry, SLS can be used for literacy improvement. The scope of this project is, thus, extensive, considering that India has the máximum number of non- and neo-literates in the world. Such large numbers can only be reached on a sustained basis through the mass media. When the fractional cost of SLS is put together with its potential for mass reading skill upgradation as a lifelong process, it can be expected to attract the attention of policy-makers.

■ Implementation Difficulties

If SLS is to be implemented in a broadcast mode, it has to resonate with top policy-makers in the media and education, simultaneously. So far this has not been possible either at the centre (New Delhi) or in the three major states that have been approached with some seriousness, i.e., Gujarat, Rajasthan and Madhya Pradesh. One of the reasons for this situation is that media and education policy-making are now increasingly on independent paths. Doordarshan[5] (DD) is burdened with pressures to compete and raise its own resources while policy-makers in education are reluctant to pay for experimentation. Consequently, the other option seems to be to approach the corporate sector or international donors to help in proving the merit of SLS in pilot projects and then persuading policy-makers to pay for implementation. But, international donors are equally reluctant to fund such pilot projects that require considerable commitment from policy-makers for implementation.

In New Delhi, both DD and the NLM have shown a lukewarm response, though slightly better response was felt at some state levels. In Gujarat, the Doordarshan Kendra (DDK) at Ahmedabad expressed interest to experiment in a live pilot project, provided the finance for subtitling and research could be worked out. However, the education policy-making in Gujarat has so far not expressed an interest in financing such an initiative unless the idea is 'proved'. In Rajasthan, education policy-making expressed interest, but has not been able to evoke the interest of NLM. DDK in Rajasthan, too, did not pay much attention to the idea since it lacked the commercial component. Education policy-makers in Madhya Pradesh responded positively, however, the discussion is yet in the preliminary stage.

The most hopeful scenario for a long-term pilot project is in Gujarat, because of the willingness of the present leadership in DDK, Ahmedabad, and also the experimental and collaborative spirit demonstrated by the leadership at the Developmental Education and Communication Unit (DECU) of the Indian Space Research Organization (ISRO). What remains to be done, now, is carrying out a sustained pilot project in broadcast mode. If SLS continues to show the same benefits already found in the controlled experiment, a strategy to implement it sustainably on a national scale needs to be evolved. SLS offers colossal gains from a small change in existing television programmes. This 'small change' itself requires little finance as compared to the budget of the NLM for post-literacy development. Ironically, while the national scale of potential benefits to literacy through SLS may qualify for consideration by heavy-duty funding agencies, because the funding requirement itself is so minuscule, the idea may not fall under their purview.

Objections to the use of film culture for literacy skill development have also been raised as film songs come in a variety of moral hues and shades. Even though the recent turn is towards the risqué, there are numerous songs that are acceptable both visually and lyrically to the general masses. The context for implementing SLS, as suggested, is in programmes that are already being televized. This is occurring in an informal home ambience and not a formal educational one. Merely by subtitling existing programmes, one cannot dramatically alter their cultural implications. Hence, resistance to SLS of film songs on the basis that it may lead to a degeneration of values seems to be a specious argument. The battle against *filmi* culture on moral grounds has proved to be a major stumbling block for some policy-makers.

Some policy-makers seem to be uncertain as to whether the neo-literate would read the subtitles at all. But studies have established in a series of rigorous experiments using eyeball movement tracking that reading of subtitles is an 'automatic' and 'mandatory' process that takes place, 'independently of familiarity with subtitling and the availability of a sound track' (Van de Poel and d'Ydewalle 1999). The field tests endorsed that viewers watching subtitled programmes were more likely to sing along or lip-sync. Although this fact has been strongly supported by several studies, the genuine willingness to weigh the evidence of literature and field studies against a personal hunch is often weak.

The SLS project for television inspired yet another context of songs for the integration of ICT, popular culture and literacy development. In contrast to film songs, produced by a select few and fed to the masses unidirectionally, the 'stills in sync' project draws upon people's creativity for people's 'edutainment'.

■ Stills in Sync with People's Songs of Change

Folk songs, past and present, represent the cultural energy of a community. They are as much an echo of the deep-seated values, beliefs and attitudes of the people as they are compasses for social change and action. Far from being a cultural energy frozen in time, folk songs are a dynamic mode of social change. The present effort focuses on cutting-edge folk songs, i.e., songs that specifically address issues across the social spectrum, including, but not limited to, the environment, natural resources, sustainable agriculture, women's issues, health, primary education, human rights and child labour.

At the lower budgetary end, folk songs could be recorded on audio tapes and at the higher end, they could be shot on video or film. This project implements a visualization method that lies in between by recreating an audio-visual experience of folk songs with the help of still images (slides/photographs), SLS (song-phrase subtitles), and the song itself. The communication experience involves showing the appropriately subtitled stills when the song is being played. We shall call this communication technique 'stills in sync" (SIS).

Several considerations make SIS a potentially useful technique. Compared to video and film, it is a relatively inexpensive approach to visually document folk songs and lends itself to participatory visualization/documentation. Through SLS, the approach draws greater attention to the lyrics and meaning while encouraging literacy skill development, memorization and vocabulary enhancement as an incidental learning process. In formal educational contexts, SIS is more acceptable than SLS of film songs.

SIS was first implemented on slides in four straightforward steps by:

- Writing down the phrases of a given song;
- taking photographs to visualize each song-phrase with inputs from the writer/singer;
- subtitling photographs with the associated song-phrase; and
- shooting the subtitled photographs individually on slide film.

A folk song thus produced could then be shown with a slide projector and the accompanying song played on a cassette player. So far, 15 songs of change have been implemented on slides. However, the mechanical difficulties with slide projectors and the expense of duplicating songs on slide has made it more viable to implement the songs on CD-ROM or television.

SIS on television and CD-ROM: The project has veered towards creating digital audio-video files (AVI) of the songs so that these may be available both on video or stored on a CD-ROM. The video is useful for broadcast on television and the CD-ROM can be used in schools and/or other contexts with access to computers, in a jukebox interface permitting song selection. Subtitling in these songs has been designed to change colour in sync with the word that is being sung. This approach is thought to bring some movement to, what is otherwise, a succession of still images. From a reading improvement perspective, the still images enable the eye to follow the colour change in the text.

SIS for plays and stories: The SIS approach can be adapted to plays and stories. For instance, one of the street plays of World Vision of India, aimed at increasing the enrolment of slum children in schools, was documented on slide. The underlying rationale for the use of SIS is that it is a veritable task, logistically, to have the whole group of actors together, every time a play is staged. While street plays would definitely evoke greater enthusiasm, the advantage of SIS is that they can be shown by just one person in a variety of contexts and far more frequently.

Research directions for SIS: Research will focus on the effectiveness of SIS for development communication. Specifically it will look at people-to-people learning of social issues, in and across village contexts. A content analysis of the songs/plays will be undertaken to learn about local priorities of social change and 'development'. Once a reasonable stock of songs is ready, literacy gains due to SLS will be explored in a school or adult education setting where repeated viewing of SIS is possible. An attempt is being made to broadcast the songs on television in educational and non-educational programming. Cross-learning between urban and rural children, in terms of awareness about each other's expressions of change, will be assessed.

SIS presents a fertile ground for experimentation. The method has the potential to conserve local culture by providing a creative incentive to people. Simultaneously, SIS offers a way to tap people's cultural energy for learning and social action.

■ Concluding Remarks

Ultimately, the benefits of SLS/SIS should be evaluated by the end users, i.e., the neo-literates in this case. Extensive field tests have underlined a positive response by them. Ironically, the decision makers are likely to judge the usefulness of the technique from a 'literate' perspective. A neo-literate's gratification in being able to read cannot be experienced by a literate person. Hence, it would be advisable to let neo-literates have the final say on whether or not it should be implemented in a broadcast mode.

Notes

1. Ashok Joshi and Kanu Patel have also contributed to this paper.
2. A neo-literate is defined here as someone who is not irreversibly literate.
3. *Chitrahaar* is the first film-song based-television programme of its kind initiated by Doordarshan. Still very popular, it is a half an hour programme that is currently broadcast two times a week.
4. Photograph by Mr Jaladhi Pujara.
5. Doordarshan is a national and state television. National-level broadcasting comes under the purview of the Directorate General of Doordarshan in New Delhi. Responsibility for state-level broadcasting in vernaculars falls under the Doordarshan Kendras (DDKs) in most states.

References

Athreya, Venkatesh B. and **Chunkath, Sheela Rani**, 1996, *Literacy and Empowerment*, Sage Publications, New Delhi.

Kothari, Brij, 1998, Film Songs as Continuing Education: Same Language Subtitling for Literacy, *Economic and Political Weekly*, 33(39), pp. 2507–10.

Report of Expert Group, 1994, Evaluation of Literacy Campaign in India, National Literacy Mission, New Delhi.

Sinha, Arbind, and **Parmar, K.M.**, 1995, INSAT Effects Study. Television and Rural Life: A Closer Look. Development and Educational Communication Unit and Indian Space Research Organization. Technical Report, ISRO-DECU-TR-106-95, Ahmedabad and Bangalore.

Van de Poel, Marijke and **d'Ydewalle, Gery**, 1999, Incidental Foreign Language Acquisition by Children Watching Subtitled Television Programs, *Journal of Psycholinguistic Research*, forthcoming.

15

Multipurpose Electronics and Computer Centres: Promoting IT Centred Maintenance and Employment in Rural Areas

SANTOSH CHOUBEY

Since 1995, the All India Society for Electronics and Computer Technology (AISECT) has been implementing an All India Coordinated Programme (AICP) to set up multipurpose electronics and computer centres in rural and tribal areas of the country. The programme, jointly funded by the department of electronics (DoE) and the department of science and technology (DST), is being implemented in 10 states. Today over 600 training, servicing and production centres have been set up under this programme, and a large variety of training and servicing modules have been prepared in the vernacular languages. Entrepreneurship in the field of electronics and information technology has also been nurtured. Interesting new possibilities related to village information centres, village communication centres, agricultural electronics applications, Geographical Information Systems (GIS) and medical electronics maintenance have come up. A national organizational structure is now in place. Ten regional centres have been set up with the support of the DoE in collaboration with the national centre, which is being run by AISECT. This paper reviews the impact of the AICP, draws some conclusions regarding implementing the rural centres and finally suggests future directions for the centres.

■ Key Ideas

The focus has to be rural: The major thrust of developmental programmes has to be on rural areas since that is where more than three-fourths of the Indian population resides. Of the 50 major cities, 500 districts, 5,000 blocks, 3,000 watersheds, 100,000 panchayats and 700,000 villages in India, the AICP's focus is at the block, watershed and panchayat levels.

Rural centres have to be multipurpose: Rural intervention in electronics and information technology has to be multipurpose in order to yield optimum results. As far as possible it should undertake training and servicing of technologies such as computers (hardware and software), consumer electronics, electrical items, telecommunications and other support services, such as institutional and programmatic linkages (see Table 15.1).

While establishing a centre, the following should be kept in mind.

Start with training: Starting with training has several advantages. It creates awareness about the centre and about the technology, and makes the centre self-sustaining from the very beginning.

Multipurpose: A single activity like production may neither render a rural centre economically viable nor put the technology to optimum use. Therefore the centres have to be multipurpose. 'Training-cum-servicing' coupled with 'production' can produce optimum results.

Effective linkages: The centre has to link up with rural institutions, such as educational institutions, banks, development departments, panchayats and health centres.

Innovative: The centre should be innovative in its choices of courses, training methodology and marketing specific to the circumstances of the area.

Sustainable: The centre should be sustainable within a short (two-three years) time period.

Language: As far as possible all the training material has to be in the regional language.

■ Methodology for Setting Up a Multipurpose Electronics and IT Centre

Setting up a centre requires initial financial support and linkages with other institutions. The cost, on an average, of setting up a centre has been

Table 15.1 Application areas for multipurpose centres

Computers	Hardware: maintenance, installation, support
Computers	Software: development, installation, maintenance, support, marketing
Consumer electronics	Audio, video, household appliances, servicing, marketing support
Communications	Telephone instruments, STD/PCO, battery chargers, exchanges, MARR equipment servicing, installation, maintenance
Electrical items	Power supply items, pumps and motors, household appliances, electrical wing
Support services	Software development, training, institutional and programmatic linkages

around \$4,760 (Rs 2 lakhs), which includes a computer laboratory, an electronics and electrical laboratory, software and furniture. Recurring costs during the first year are around \$3,100 (Rs 1.33 lakhs). This includes manpower, rent and consumable items.

Steps to Set Up a Centre

This begins with a preliminary survey, data analysis and selection of a nodal point, and then proceeds to procuring and installing equipment. Household and market surveys are conducted typically along with setting up the servicing and production functions of the centre. Centres then diversify into other areas and institutional activities. They become viable in their second year of operation.

■ Interlinkages with Institutions

Various organizations/departments are now linked to the centres providing support services. These include, to name a few, the state electronics development corporations, the National Open School, Indira Gandhi National Open University, NABARD, departments of rural development, and voluntary organizations such as the Society for Rural Industrialization, the Centre for Quantitative Research and the Institute of Vocational Training.

■ Experience in Block-level Centres

The AICP was funded by the DoE and the DST. The programme was designed to set up 10 block-level multipurpose centres as nodal points in 10 states. In addition, a large number of 'entrepreneurial' centres were to be set up on a self-financing basis. Supporting course-ware and training material were produced for the centres, and 10 per cent of the total funds were provided by the government.

Of the 633 centres established under the AICP, over 420 are in rural areas. The largest number of centres are in Madhya Pradesh (495) followed by Maharashtra (44), Uttar Pradesh (36), Rajasthan (20), Bihar (11), Orissa and Gujarat (9 each), Andhra Pradesh (3), Tamil Nadu/Pondicherry (4), and Kerala and Delhi (1 each). Each centre provides direct employment to four to five persons (as trainers and technicians) and indirect employment to another two to three persons. For this, the centre has to invest about $3,570 to $4,760 (Rs 1.5 to Rs 2.05 lakhs). The centres generate employment for over 2,000 persons. The annual turnover per centre on the average is about $2,380 (Rs 1.02 lakhs). The total network turnover is around $1,428,571 (Rs 614 lakhs).

To enable the centres to be multipurpose, most of the technical material for training, servicing and production has been developed in local languages. The training modules include training material on computers and electronics in Hindi as well as in the regional languages. Service manuals in Hindi include literature on servicing audio-video and telecommunications equipment. Production 'profiles' include the production of audio-video equipment, electronic hobby kits and project plans to set up small-scale electronic and electrical production units.

Various activities are conducted at the centres including training, services and production. Training includes audio-video repair, electric/electronic repair and use of computer applications. Certificates and diplomas are offered in electronics and computer applications. Training (the use of computers) is provided to bank employees, members of panchayats and other elected bodies, women involved in specified programmes and in schools. About 60 per cent of the students are based in rural areas, of which, 3,490 are males and 1,425 are females.

The production unit of a centre includes the production of power supply items, electronic entertainment items, desktop publishing and screen printing, and word and data processing. Services offered are in software development, hardware maintenance, communication centres, IT applications, artisan development and consultancy.

In addition to employment opportunities, the centres have shown to be beneficial in other ways as well. For instance:

- Over 20,000 school children are being trained under the computer literacy programme.
- A panchayat planning information system for 20 panchayats of one watershed is under development.
- Maintenance centres have been set up to provide telecommunications services.
- Core groups on agriculture and medical electronics have been formed.
- Various new roles, such as becoming employment bureaus and community libraries are emerging to enhance the effectiveness of rural centres.

- Centres act as retail outlets for electronic consumables.

■ Conclusions

The following conclusions have arisen from implementing these centres:

- A multipurpose approach with regard to block/sub-block level electrical–electronics–computer centres turned out to be an important and appropriate concept. Besides training, the centres have to take up servicing and production activities. Within the training segment too, there is a demand in areas other than electrical–electronics and computer fields.
- It is difficult to organize production in rural centres without a continuous support system.
- There is demand for designing short-term courses directly related to various vocations. An example is training programmes for the repair and maintenance of the STD/PCO telecommunications equipment.
- There is a demand for certifying existing skills.
- Production work can be facilitated by preparing production profiles, production and testing documents, and providing sourcing for small entrepreneurs.
- Instructions in Hindi or the regional language play a vital role in teaching technical subjects.
- The training package on electronics entrepreneurship was helpful in orienting prospective entrepreneurs and in setting up new multipurpose centres.
- Networking of the centres is required to share information and resources.
- Greater participation of women in the centres should be encouraged.
- Some centres have found new roles for themselves as village information centres.
- Maintenance of specialized computer and communications items require strengthening support systems and a higher training input.

■ Linkages with Other Voluntary Groups, Government and Public Bodies

The AISECT has linked the centres with voluntary groups, government departments of science and technology, electronics, telecommunications, non-conventional energy sources, state electronics corporations, industries, education, panchayat, women and child, and health, as well as with agro-industries, banks, schools and colleges.

■ Rural Electronics Entrepreneurship Development Programme

The AISECT has been conducting an Electronics Entrepreneurship Development Programme to motivate and mobilize rural youth to set up their own training and service centres. It also guides youth in methods and means to obtain financial support from various institutions.

Spread over 10 days, the programme includes sessions on the world and the Indian scenario of electronics and information technology, entrepreneurship, identification of local needs, market surveys, procedures involved in obtaining assistance, management, accounts, roles of a centre, establishing a centre, and linking it with various organizations.

■ Future Directions

The multipurpose electronics and IT centres described here provide a possible model for replication in all 5,000 blocks of the country. It is more useful at the block and sub-block level where IT is not widely diffused. The centre's financial viability and utility have been shown in over 600 centres. Further expansion would require institutional support and strengthening of the national as well as regional centres. The AISECT is developing a model for IT-based panchayat resource centres, which can act as a basis for knowledge-based planning and management in rural areas. Plans are underway to double the number of centres, many of which will become Internet service providers (ISPs).

PART VI

Conclusion

16

Emerging State-level ICT Development Strategies

RAJA MITRA

In recent years various state governments of India have formulated ICT strategies. Karnataka was the first state to present an IT policy in 1997 to attract private investment. Several others followed suit. Maharasthra and Tamil Nadu have been successful in attracting private investors to software exports and in implementing local ICT projects. Andhra Pradesh has emerged as a role model for state IT policy designed to both attract private investment and deliver public sector projects that improve services to citizens. So far, state ICT policy (and the national IT policy) have focused on international, national, statewide and urban dimensions—the rural dimension is noted as being important in such policies but is not a focus in terms of committed resources. This paper analyzes the growing role of state governments in ICT development—including opportunities and strategic and management challenges. There is ample scope for states to learn from each other in terms of general policy and specific projects. Late and early starter strategies are discussed to ensure sustainable competitiveness and to develop specific niches of comparative advantage.

■ Introduction

New technologies and the human and institutional capacity building of the past decade in the public and private sectors, coupled with trends towards a greater emphasis on development initiatives at the state level, have resulted in a paradigm shift in the roles of the private sector, central and state governments in terms of ICT. As demonstrated in Karnataka, Maharasthra, Tamil Nadu and Andhra Pradesh, concerted local, private and/or state government initiatives can make a major difference in terms of the development of the ICT sector. These developments appear to imply a shift away from the past centralized public sector led investments towards decentralization in which the private sector and state governments play major roles.

Though the IT applications in various states were initiated 10–20 years ago, it is only in recent years that the state governments have begun to formulate their own strategies to develop the IT sector (Government of Tamil Nadu 1997; Government of Maharashtra 1998; Government of Andhra Pradesh 1999). Realizing the importance of concerted strategies to cope with rapid growth in the ICT sector and to compete with other states for more private investment, Karnataka was the first state to present a state IT policy. Since then, several states have followed suit. Andhra Pradesh has now emerged as the principal role model for state IT policy not only in terms of attracting private investment but also in terms of public sector ICT policy and projects.

Previously the use of IT in the government sector was dominated by central government programmes, such as those implemented by the National Informatics Centre (NIC), and ad hoc efforts of the departments or agencies at the state level. At present, there is a greater emphasis on initiatives driven and managed by the state governments. This may include both stand alone and multipurpose ICT project plans. Karnataka, for example, has for a long time, initiated IT in the government sector although these efforts were by and large made on an ad hoc basis at the departmental or agency level (Government of Karnataka 1997).

■ Emerging State IT Policy

In May 1998, the central government adopted the national taskforce's recommendation that each state government should develop an IT policy (Government of India 1998b). Each department in the central and state government would be required to prepare five-year IT plans. About 1–3 per cent of the budget of every ministry/department would be earmarked for incorporating IT. This investment includes not only the cost of IT hardware and software, but also training and external procurement of IT services. The heads of the respective departments have been empowered to re-appropriate budget for these services (Government of India 1998a, 1998b, 1999).

Since then as many as 14 out of 26 state governments have set up their own IT departments. The primary objective of these departments is to promote investments in software, hardware and telecommunications. Emphasis is placed on increasing in-house implementation and use of IT in the government sector for the benefit of citizens.

■ Factors Driving IT Strategies

The importance given to ICT policy and projects by the central and state governments as well as by the private sector has encouraged the rapid growth of IT sector in India, both in terms of the external surge in software exports and growth in the domestic market. Leading representatives of the private sector have been highly proactive in formulating strategies and action plans for the central and state governments and for the national IT taskforce. Today it is widely recognized that IT combined with advances in communication technologies is emerging as a key factor in private and public sector led social and economic development efforts for national and state-level governments as well as for urban and rural society.

The acceleration of efforts to develop state-level strategies can be explained by:

- The increased demand for ICT at local levels and the limitation of the centralized approaches in meeting this demand effectively. The rapid expansion of the Internet and telecommunication connectivity, including the introduction of cable, wireless service and various new emerging technologies such as satellite and web-TV communication systems offer new opportunities in term of a widespread diffusion of ICT;
- growth of the IT industry in certain cities such as Bangalore, Mumbai, Delhi, Chennai and Hyderabad;
- the momentum generated by the national IT taskforce, and the fact that the new policies at the centre have been designed in close collaboration with the state governments, the IT industry and researchers. This style of policy development is in stark contrast to the old planning variety;
- IT industry associations such as the National Association of Software and Services Companies (NASSCOM), the Manufacturers Association for Information Technology (MAIT), the Confederation of Indian Industry (CII), and other private business groups actively lobby the government to promote the growth of IT industry. In several states, private business associations, such as the CII and local chambers of commerce, have formulated proposals for state IT policy.

■ Key Components

The state IT policy focuses on the following:

- Promotion of private investment: Investment will be encouraged through promotional activities and incentive schemes (including taxation and finance).
- Investment in physical infrastructure: This includes investments in physical infrastructure and facilities relating to IT such as land and real estate development, power and water, roads and air transport, telecommunication and Internet connectivity and industrial parks (public or private sector investment and operation).
- Investment in human resources: Investment in human resources includes research, education and training.
- Development of governmental IT applications and content: Development of IT applications and content in the government sector (rural and urban) includes the identification and implementation of application projects in various sectors.

Thus so far, state ICT policy has focused on the international, national and statewide urban dimensions. Though the rural dimension has been accepted as very important in terms of economic and development rationale, it is not the primary focus in terms of resource allocation. The private sector investments tend to focus on one or two urban clusters in the state while little or no resources are diverted to rural and backward areas.

■ Mechanisms to Implement State IT Policy

Several states have identified institutions/departments that will work as a 'think tank' to produce a vision of how IT will be deployed in the state. Most of the states have created a separate IT department headed by a senior administrator. Some, like Gujarat, have also appointed a minister for IT, and an adviser with a ministerial rank.

Clear champions have, however, not emerged. Several senior-level bureaucrats who are IT literate or have experience in implementing IT projects are keen to take on the mantle of a champion, irrespective of the department that they may be heading. Only Andhra Pradesh has a clear demarcation of responsibility and a legitimized champion.

Most state governments have created a separate organization to implement the infrastructure development plans. Infrastructure development has two key components: creation of a statewide area network which is likely to benefit rural IT projects and creation of technology parks to attract investments by IT companies. The technology parks are being planned on lines similar to the ones established by the centre.

The central government played a catalytic role in establishing software technology parks (STPs) in several states set up by the government's department of electronics (DoE) in 1991 as a non-profit society to promote and facilitate software exports. The STPs have expanded in terms of numbers and scope of services provided in each park. STP software exports for 1999–2000 are expected to reach over $350 million (Rs 1,505 crores approx.).

The STP 'Vision—2002' plan envisages enhancing software exports from the STPs 10 times by the year 2002. To accomplish this, major investments in STP infrastructure are planned. These include increasing the capacity of the existing satellite earth stations and establishing new stations in Chennai, Jaipur, Mohali and Navi Mumbai. It would also promote software industry exports in 20 more cities by establishing new communications infrastructure and buildings for software firms.

Not much thought is being given to the regional dispersion of IT industry in planning the state technology parks. In this sense the development of the IT industry will continue to be an enclave phenomena concentrated in certain large cities. While the IT industry in city clusters is growing and undergoing structural change, it is characterized by limited linkages to other parts of the urban economy and has even less linkages to rural areas and backward states.

Learning from past experience, multi-pronged inputs such as venture capital and incubator training centres are being planned as part of the technology parks. The spectrum of activities that the park infrastructure will support is likely to widen to software services such as data entry, web design and e-commerce.

Another key component of the implementation plan is the setting up of new educational institutions to augment the manpower supply. As many as four state-level institutes of information technology have already been created and a few others are on the anvil. In many of these institutions, Indian private sector companies have shown a great deal of interest in collaborating with the government. In Karnataka, a private sector company was initially involved in building, operating and transferring a working institution. In Gujarat, a private sector company has offered to participate in the equity of the new institute. Interestingly, the structure of the new institutes have varied from a section 20 private company, a non-profit society, to a traditional organizational form of a centre entirely supported by the state/central government. However, the increasing trend of private participation is visible.

■ Commonalties and Differences in State IT Policy

The IT policy of different states has many elements in common. In some there are striking similarities even in the text. For example, Punjab's IT strategy draws heavily on documents produced by the Andhra Pradesh government. While there are many similarities in state IT policy, there are also notable differences in their content and management aspects, including:

- The emphasis placed on the four principal components of IT policy mentioned earlier. Karnataka's IT strategy emphasizes overcoming existing acute bottlenecks in physical infrastructure. Andhra Pradesh, on the other hand, focuses on developing governmental IT applications and communication networks.
- Most states in the eastern region place emphasis on the requirements of a 'late starter' such as basic computer awareness, training and attracting existing Indian IT firms to establish branches. They also tend to focus on developing new IT industrial parks and invigorating existing parks. There have been examples in the past where IT-oriented industrial parks have failed. Bhubaneshwar in Orissa and Ahmedabad in Gujarat were two of the first cities to have an STP, but for many years failed to attract investors. IT states which are 'early starters' tend to focus on developing high-end education, infrastructure facilities, and attracting multinational investors (e.g., Bangalore). These differences are also reflected in the development of new IT clusters within a state such as Mysore and Mangalore in the case of Karnataka.
- The capacity and commitment to formulate, manage and implement IT policy effectively at all levels of government. States like Andhra Pradesh and Tamil Nadu have an explicit and comprehensive IT policy with a strong commitment towards implementation. In some states the development of government IT applications to a

large extent stems from ad hoc initiatives at the departmental level. The degree of inter-governmental coordination and collaboration differs significantly among states. In many cases the capacity to implement government IT applications is especially weak in rural areas.

New policies are emerging rapidly both at the central and state level. It is, however, too early to undertake substantive analysis of state IT policy, their implementation and likely impact. In many states IT policy is in preliminary stages; other states are yet to present an IT policy. The policies have often been compiled rather quickly and appear to be declarations of intent with little scope or hope of being implemented. There is an apparent need to foster cross-fertilization of experiences among different states in terms of design, finance and implementation of policy interventions and projects.

■ Salient Features in State-level Success and Failure in ICT Development

Broadly speaking, states fall into the following two categories: (*a*) early starters which now have a significant, well-established IT industry; and (*b*) late starters or lagers in terms of having a stable IT industry.

The early starters are states which are more dynamic in terms of development of manufacturing and modern services industries, as also in attracting investments both from India and abroad. Late starters lag behind in terms of having a sizeable absolute growth in other modern industrial and service sectors and in attracting investments. Early starters with a significantly developed IT industry displayed stronger performance in terms of general economic growth and several other development indicators as compared to the late starters. This pattern, however, does not apply uniformly. A state in the earlier stages may be in the starter category but still be a moderate performer in terms of certain social indicators such as literacy and health or rural development. Conversely, a state in the late starter category may have a strong record in higher education (West Bengal), or literacy and health indicators (Kerala).

States in the early starter category are not necessarily the ones with the most comprehensive approach in terms of formulating and implementing state IT policy interventions and projects. Until recently, states such as Karnataka and Maharashtra did not have an IT policy. The boom in the IT software industry in these states has been driven by the private sector. On the other hand, late starters such as Andhra Pradesh, Kerala and Punjab are emerging as states that strongly emphasize a concerted effort to develop the IT industry with the state government playing a major, proactive role.

The early starters which now have the largest IT industry are the two states of Maharasthra and Karnataka. Mumbai and Bangalore have the largest IT industries among Indian cities, followed by Chennai and Delhi. Bangalore has been looked upon as a role model. It has attracted a large number of private investors from other states as well as from foreign countries. It now has a significant export-oriented IT industry. Here the IT software industry has developed due to initiatives of the private sector. The pattern for Mumbai and Pune is similar; both cities have strong potential to develop linkages with the large local modern industry and service sector.

Tamil Nadu, too, is attracting private investment because of the stable and strong commitment of the government to develop the IT sector, even before it presented a state IT policy. Moreover, the government has made significant progress in terms of concerted efforts to develop ICT for the public sector.

■ Late Starter in Terms of Having a Significant IT Industry

Late starters include states such as Andhra Pradesh, West Bengal, Orissa, Kerala, Gujarat and Punjab as well as industrially less developed states such as Assam, Tripura and Manipur.

A comparison between Hyderabad and Calcutta provides a striking contrast: the former has rapidly developed the IT sector, despite its weak industry, commerce and knowledge institutions and networks. Traditionally, Calcutta has been rich in industry, trading, and knowledge institutions and networks, but it is lagging behind other metros in private investment growth as well as expansion of graduate education and technology research programmes. Although West Bengal has certain apparent comparative advantages in developing an IT industry, such as a large number of people with high educational qualifications, its role as the leading industrial, commercial and cultural centre in the eastern region, and its low cost of land and real estate as compared to Bangalore, Delhi and Mumbai, it has a poor reputation in work culture, labour relations and development of modern physical infrastructure.

Andhra Pradesh has proven that a strongly committed and effective government can make a major difference in developing the ICT sector. Moreover, Andhra Pradesh policies have been characterized by a strong emphasis on development of the ICT sector in partnership with the private sector and consulting expertise in India and abroad.

There is no uniform pattern or single model for success. There is ample scope for states to learn from each other's experience both in terms of general policy and specific projects. Late starters may benefit from the experiences of an early starter. They need to take into account the difference in timing, competitive situation and technology available. Early starters can also learn from each other but the conditions among late starters may also differ radically. Developing the IT sector in West Bengal differs substantially from doing this in a small state like Tripura dominated by traditional economic sectors.

■ Common Determinants of Poor Performance and Success

Efforts to develop the ICT sector have been marked by either success or by complete or partial failures. Key reasons for the poor performance include deficiencies in:

- Well-defined policy objectives and strategic approach;
- management of projects in terms of design and implementation;
- finance mobilization and management;
- human resource development and management;
- institutional and thereby related generic structural problems in government; and
- staying power and commitment to implement policies and projects effectively.

Though these are the common drawbacks at all levels of government, they do not apply uniformly. Some central and state government departments are in a fairly good position to counter such challenges while others may have a long way to go. In addition, there are weaknesses in the strategic approach taken by some states to develop the ICT sector. These include the inability to foster linkages between the development of ICT in urban and rural areas, to attract private investment in ICT, to promote public–private sector partnerships, and to tap lessons from the experiences of other states in India and abroad.

The initiatives of the central government in appointing a national taskforce to give a new direction to the IT policy is likely to have a far-reaching impact on the developments of ICT in India. The recommendations of the national IT taskforce that have been accepted by the union government in a large measure are now percolating down to the state level. As has been mentioned earlier, several state governments have formulated their own IT policy. Even though the documents may show a lot of commonality, actual progress on implementation is likely to be substantially different. States that are considered to be well-governed and have a demonstrated ability in implementing developmental programmes, are also likely to be more successful in implementing IT policy. The degree of success of implementation is of course dependant on the kind of resources state governments are able to mobilize to push the development of IT infrastructure, as well as the use of IT at the level of the state governments. The two sources that most state governments are trying to tap are multilateral aid agencies and the private sector in India. Some states such as Andhra Pradesh and Uttar Pradesh have been successful in receiving large loans for their IT projects. However, the degree of success in attracting private investments either from multinational or Indian companies has been fairly low. Only Andhra Pradesh has met with some success. This state has collaborated with large Indian companies such as L&T, and has also been able to attract many multinationals in the field of education.

■ Conclusion

Whether the state-level IT policy will impact on the process of development of rural areas is yet to be seen. In about the next five years, the policies are likely to impact the process of dispensing tax collection and other government services in urban towns. Perhaps the data networking and the communication infrastructure may reach the *taluka* level during this period. Any large-scale deployment of IT at the *taluka* level and below is likely to happen only after five years or so. The strongest impact of the state-level policy of IT will be in the creation of awareness amongst the bureaucracy as well as in the expansion of the pool of trained manpower available to implement IT projects at the state levels.

References

Government of Andhra Pradesh. 1999, A Premier IT Centre of India, Andhra Pradesh: Vision 2020, Andhra Pradesh.

Government of India, 1998a, Information Technology Action Plan, Part I—Software. National Taskforce on Information Technology and Software Development, New Delhi.

————— 1998b, Information Technology Action Plan, Part II—Hardware. National Taskforce on Information Technology and Software Development, New Delhi.

—————. 1999, Information Technology Action Plan, Part III—Long Term National IT Policy. National Taskforce on Information Technology and Software Development, New Delhi.

Government of Karnataka, 1997, Information Technology Policy of Karnataka 1997. Proceedings of the Government of Karnataka, Karnataka.

Government of Maharashtra, 1998, Maharashtra's Information Technology Policy, Maharashtra.

Government of Tamil Nadu, 1997, Information Technology Policy of Tamil Nadu, Tamil Nadu.

17

Useful Starting Points for Future Projects

ROBERT SCHWARE

It is hardly possible to overrate the value, in the present low state of human improvement, of placing human beings in contact with persons dissimilar to themselves, and with modes of thought and action unlike those with which they are familiar. Such communication has always been, and is peculiarly in the present age, one of the primary sources of progress.

John Stuart Mill, *Principles of Political Economy*, vol. 3 (1848)

■ ICT and Economic Development

The ICT sector as a whole (telecommunications, broadcasting, computer hardware and software, and related technologies) has emerged as a strategically important sector driving social and economic change in India. Already television and radio are ubiquitous communication technologies. In the last few years there has also been a significant surge in terms of access to telephony, Internet and computers, although starting from a very low base.

The IT industry is moving up the value-added chain. It is expanding its focus beyond lower-end software service and body-shopping to a wide range of areas such as development of packages, electronic commerce and Internet applications, enterprise resource planning, and various IT-enabling services for the private and public sector in India and abroad. Software is expected to emerge as India's number one export earner within a few years. Simultaneously, the hardware industry could expand to a turnover of US$30 billion (approx. Rs 1,29,000 crores) by 2008. This would make IT a major sector in the Indian economy worth about US$100 billion (Rs 4,30,100 crores) or close to 8 per cent of the country's GDP in the year 2008. The software export industry alone would provide jobs to more than 1.5 million software professionals, contribute to more than one-quarter of the country's total exports earnings, and constitute close to 4 per cent of GDP. Envisaged growth targets for the ITC sector may not be achieved in full due to infrastructure, human resource, capital and other constraints. However, it appears clear that ICT will grow rapidly, especially since it is in many respects an infant or nascent industry in the country (computer, telephony and Internet use is still very low on a per capita basis). The prime minister's launching of a national IT taskforce in 1998 marks a beginning of a new chapter in the history of India's ICT sector and its role in the economy. The work of the taskforce has demonstrated the need to give high priority to a wide-range of policy reforms and to substantially increase public and private investments relating to the ICT sector. These developments seem to suggest that ICT could improve the context for social and economic change in the domestic economy, including rural areas, and the management of the public sector. The donor community, too, is seeking a more active role in participating in this process.

There is a debate on prioritization in the social and economic development agenda. While the need for major investment in support of the development of the modern urban ICT sector, including software exports, is widely accepted, there is an ongoing debate on how to balance the need to give priority to investment targeting basic needs such as primary education, basic health services, water and sanitation requirements versus ICT. This debate applies to the whole country, and rural and backward areas in particular. Some argue that the priority in rural areas should be given to basic needs such as primary education and health, water and sanitation and not to modern ICT such as computers and Internet connectivity. Others argue that the focus of ICT in rural areas should be on basic telephony, and broadcasting through radio and TV rather than computerization and Internet connectivity. There are still others who argue that new technologies such as low cost web-TV, and opportunities for technological leapfrogging in connectivity, by directly investing in satellite-based communication systems and new ICT application and content relevant to the demand in rural areas, could drastically improve the delivery of information-related services to citizens, agricultural extension services, and provision of health and social services.

I have been fascinated by the lack of evidence from other countries and case study material from India itself in these debates. Recently, for instance, the expansion of telecommunications into rural areas saw declining price differentials between cocoa sold to Ivorian middlemen and in London commodity markets (Bond 1997). In Sri Lanka, the price received by farmers for their products jumped from 50 to 60 per cent of the

Colombo price before the introduction of rural telephones to 80 to 90 per cent in the aftermath of the telephone service rollout (Saunders et al. 1983). These are just a few examples of telecommunications in rural areas allowing for better and more rapid decision making amongst a wider range of alternatives with reduced transaction costs.

■ Implications of the Case Studies

The case studies in this book have covered a lot of ground, and are useful in: (a) taking stock of current ICT applications in the rural sector in India; (b) understanding ICT's potential for impacting development in rural areas; (c) drawing lessons from experiences in using ICT for rural development; and (d) providing recommendations—from the point of view of actual practitioners—for diffusing ICT in various rural sectors. In order to find implications for rural development strategies and programmes, in these studies we search for applications of ICT in rural development (see Annotated Bibliography), and for examples of best practice.

It is fair to conclude that we have uncovered no magic wand: the cases suggest that implementing ICT in rural development projects in India will require paying attention to three key factors of success: for whom, what bundle of services (multipurpose), and how well they are managed.

■ For Whom?

A detailed understanding of the work environment of end users, needs of the beneficiaries, and specific benefits proposed to be delivered leads to well-planned and executed projects, as illustrated in the Healthcare, CARD, NDDB, and Honey Bee projects. The Healthcare pilot project in Ajmer, Rajasthan, clearly targeted the grassroots-level health worker. These auxiliary nurse midwives have direct contact with over 5,000 persons spread over several villages. I know of few ICT projects that use multidisciplinary teams from around the world to the extent of this project in project design, to ascertain how the ANMs do their jobs collecting basic demographic data, administering immunizations, family welfare, and mother–child health programmes. Their practices and priorities were well-defined, and not just official functions, but informal practices and roles within villages were also identified.

It was recognized early on in the CARD project in Andhra Pradesh that users of the IT application could effectively block efforts to automate conventional manual methods of copying, indexing, retrieving, and paying for land-related documents, and, more importantly, transforming the registration department from a highly procedure-bound office (that brought a host of corrupt practices and sent citizens to brokers) to one that is 'citizen-friendly'. A group of such users was thus selected to participate in the various tasks (and opportunities) to redesign business processes around their computer investments, rather than vice versa, and subsequently to participate in the design and development of the software. No external technical personnel were recruited, which provided a sense of system ownership and even 'control on technology' to the users within the registration department.

■ What Bundle of Services?

In terms of income and employment generation, and improving skills, an aspect that comes to the fore from the case studies is that rural ICT centres must be multipurpose in order to be economically viable. In addition to training, for example, the electronic and computer centres set up by the All India Society for Electronics and Computer Technology (AISECT) to service household appliances have gradually evolved to provide software development, hardware maintenance, printing and consulting information system development services. The mix of services and applications differ depending on the location of the centres. Training is the core activity, which enables the centres to become self-sustaining and to link up with local schools, panchayats and health centres to deliver training and develop ICT applications. Training in the use of ICT to enhance functional capacities and improve employment opportunities is also one of the several activities of the Blind People's Association, which is positioning itself to enable a new generation of persons with disabilities to become informatics users and information entrepreneurs. The use of Satcom for extension training demonstrated the necessity to share the same network by different user groups, allowing for specific topics for different locations and user groups.

■ Project Management and Sustainability Considerations

The empirical record revealed that all the projects took longer than expected. They required adjustment to underlying, unfavourable implementation conditions that usually left out incentives for performance. The gap between future project goals and realities may be closed somewhat by addressing issues such as those highlighted here.

Private Sector Involvement

The role of public–private partnership was exemplified in the successful diffusion of the ICT application in 600 milk societies through the efforts of a few private companies. In other projects such as CARD, training was completely out-sourced from a private company and the future plans of WARANA and APSWAN include significant roles for the private sector. The pilot project of DoT, VSNL and Inmarsat adds to the growing stock of field experiences that telephones in rural areas trickle socio-economic benefits to villages, and more so to poor ones, and to our understanding that public–private partnerships are required for the provisioning of telephones in rural villages.

Built-in Reviews

The ISRO-sponsored Jhabua Development Communications project in a predominantly tribal district of Madhya Pradesh was started with a specific intention to evaluate results and benefits through periodic socio-economic surveys and other instruments. This feedback is necessary to determine the quality of training and the extent of participation. Perhaps the most important information the survey revealed is that technology is not a barrier to this type of interactive talkback training delivery system, and that women are the quickest to become involved and participate actively. Changes in the social equilibrium are discernible from the survey results.

Timing Investments

The pace of growth in the field of ICT has meant that equipment provided through the various projects has rapidly become outdated, necessitating upgradation if not total replacement. This issue of sustainability is going to continue to face these as well as new projects, and provision will have to be made for unforeseen technical innovations or upgrades in order to keep equipment and usage current. Mistimed investment and procurement decisions—especially for larger projects such as CARD,

WARANA, and the *mandal* revenue offices—may result in costly and premature technological obsolescence.

Enhancing Existing Programmes

The information revolution offers great opportunities for informing and educating the poor. And without literacy, there will be no information revolution in rural areas; only information feudalism. However, such activities can be done either through new programmes with enormous expense and effort, or through enhancing existing programmes. Too often, governments have invested in ICT at high cost, but with limited results in terms of productivity and innovation. The pilot case of Same Language Subtitling of film songs on television shows how a simple and inexpensive addition to these programmes can achieve substantial literacy skill gains over a period of time, and that literacy skill development is a subconscious, fun by-product of viewing.

Ensuring Multipurpose and Multi-functionality

Although ICT costs are plummeting, and the technology is changing rapidly and becoming more powerful and integrated with an increasing number of products, there may be relatively high initial set-up and learning costs in rural areas (the technology cannot simply be plugged into the nearest electrical socket, and then switched on anywhere). Also recurrent cost implications are difficult to assess. In certain important respects, rural areas benefit from technologies that are multi-functional. The computerized postal system described in Chapter 7, for instance, handles money orders, speed post, inland and overseas mail, and postal life insurance. The NDDB milk testers reduce the time taken to ascertain the quality and fat content of milk and, with attached PCs, can now calculate and pay bills.

Defining Outcome Indicators

Successful cases demonstrated that they had specific quantitative and qualitative outcome measures. For example, the CARD project established rather high service standards, such that citizens approaching CARD counters to transfer or register deeds and pay the applicable duties would have to wait just minutes to obtain their documents. The issuance of certificates pertaining to landholdings, caste, nativity and income in Andhra

Pradesh used to take 15 to 20 days, and is targeted to be reduced to less than one hour with the help of IT. Before automation, farmers participating in NDDB's Operation Flood were paid only every 10 days, and even though they delivered milk each day they were never sure of the reliability of the manual calculations of quality and quantity by society staff. Now they are paid upon delivery of the milk and there is no hanky-panky in delivering information about quality, thereby defeating corruption. The postal application has demonstrated a 25 per cent reduction in queuing time and a 30 per cent reduction in transaction time.

Realistically Replicating Pilot Projects

Many factors affect the chances of pilot ICT projects becoming replicated. In the case of the introduction of information technology in the *mandal* revenue offices in Andhra Pradesh, this was planned to be done in a phased manner over three years. The pilot project at Mohinabad *mandal* began in April 1998, but has always been part of an overall Andhra Pradesh government IT strategy, and there are other, large sub-projects forthcoming. This introduces some certainty as to the correctness of the implementation against a moving, larger target. The costs of the pilot were financed from the government budget. On the other hand, the Healthcare pilot project in Rajasthan was a discrete experiment, financed by firms, which, despite its success, has had difficulties becoming replicated not only to other states, but even within the state. During the pilot stage, considerable financial, technical and managerial resources were employed. Subsequently, technology changed (Apple Computers stopped producing the Newton computer), some technical people moved on to new challenges, and funding for extension is now being secured.

Throughout this book we have confronted conditions and contexts in which uncommon ICTs are being used in rural areas throughout India. How well people, organizations and perhaps entire rural societies learn from the use of, and increasingly gain from access to, information processing technologies is a function of many variables, including the opportunities to make profits from greater knowledge, technology choices, physical conditions, and national, state and local priorities. Obviously, characteristics of projects vary from problem to problem, even in a given country. But, these seem to be the realities to which future development programmes funded by the national and state governments, and bi- and multilateral agencies must adjust. More case studies of success and failure from other countries would be especially welcome.

References

Bond, J., 1997, The Drivers of the Information Revolution—Cost, Computing Power, and Convergence. The Information Revolution and the Future of Telecommunications, World Bank, Washington D.C.

Saunders, R., Warford, J. and **Wellenius, B.**, 1983, Telecommunications and Economic Development, John Hopkins, Baltimore, Maryland, p. 19.

Annotated Bibliography

The bibliography is based on works published since 1995, with an emphasis on more recent reports and studies. Publications before 1995 have been included only where pertinent to the subject matter of the book.

Kenneth, Allen, et al, Survey of Rural Information Infrastructure Technologies. National Telecommunications and Information Administration (DOC), Washington, D.C. Available : Databases through 'Webspirs'
Accession Number: ED399125
ICTs can reduce the barriers of distance and space that are to the disadvantage of rural areas. This report defines a set of distinct voice, computer, and video telecommunications services; describes several rural information applications that make use of these services; and surveys various wireline and wireless systems and technologies that are being used or that might be used to deliver these services to rural areas. Rural information applications such as distance learning require a wide range of telecommunication services, but no current system or technology is capable of delivering all services. This report concludes that there are many technologies suitable for providing voice telecommunication services in rural areas. It is also technically feasible to provide advanced computer networking and video capabilities even to relatively small towns in rural areas.

Bayes, Abdul and **von Braun, Joachim,** *Village Pay Phones and Rural Poverty: Insights from a Grameen Bank Initiative in Bangladesh.* Available on http://www.zef.de/zef_deutsch/f_first.html

Bonder, Seth, 1997, Changing the Paradigm for Telemedicine Development and Evaluation: A Prospective Model-based Approach. *Socio-Economic Planning Sciences* (UK); 31:257-80.

Bradsher, Monica, 1995, Prospects and Strategies: Improving Basic Education in Developing Countries through the Use of Computer-based Information Technologies. Aguirre International, Arlington, VA, Development InfoStructure, Arlington, VA, World Learning Inc., Washington, D.C., USAID. Center for Human Capacity Development, Washington, D.C., (Sponsor).
How can computer-supported systems be used to help a developing country achieve its basic education objectives? This report provides background information and suggests strategies that might be used by USAID field missions in advising developing countries on educational technologies. Section I discusses a new paradigm for basic education, in which computer technology expands human capacity to communicate, and the desire for information is driven by individuals' self-interest. Section II discusses four types of technologies: computers; computer-based telecommunications; technologies for interactive distance learning; and educational software for stand-alone computers. The third section describes basic education problems and solutions facing three imaginary developing countries: a very poor

rural country, a somewhat industrialized but predominantly agricultural country, and a more advanced country. Section IV examines anticipated policy barriers and desirable host-country policies, while Section V discusses how to design interventions, e.g., who to include, costs, timeframe, evaluation, and best uses of USAID strength. The concluding section identifies the main characteristics of the challenge and USAID's comparative advantages to meet it.

Burgiss, Samuel, Enderson, Blaine, Brooks, Chris, Foster, Carolyn, D., and **Smith, Gary,** 1998, *Medicine without Boundaries.* Forum for Applied Research & Public Policy (FFAR), 13(2), pp. 101–05.
High-tech solutions to long-standing problems give patients in remote areas golden opportunities in medical care. The telemedicine programme at the University of Tennessee Medical Center at Knoxville is discussed.

Rammanohar Reddy, C., 1997, Information Technology for Development. *The Hindu,* June 26.

CIRDAP-Newsletter, 1997, Model Village in Rural Development (MVRD), Action research project experience highlighted at the final consultation. July, no. 68, pp. 1–4.
The project, Developing Model Villages in Rural Development (MVRD), was initiated by the Centre on Integrated Rural Development for Asia and the Pacific (CIRDAP) in 1991 in 11 member countries. The project was to test and document the process that would lead to a state where a village community is able to undertake its own development with minimum outside intervention. The main activities of the project consisted of information gathering, providing training to the villagers and organizing them into self-help groups to enable them to work together and resolve local problems. The MVRD project was implemented over a period of five years in collaboration with the CIRDAP link institutions. In May 1997, project coordinators, rural development practitioners, policy-makers, planners, local government institutions, non-governmental organizations and representatives of international agencies in Bangladesh met for a Final Consultation to evaluate the achievements of the project and recommend future courses of action.

Clarke, Audrey E., 1996, From Combines to Computers: Rural Services and Development in the Age of Information Technology. *Growth & Change [GRC]* 27(4) Fall, pp. 519–22.
Access No: 01358442 ProQuest ABI/INFORM (R) Global
From Combines to Computers: Rural Services and Development in the Age of Information Technology by Amy K. Glasmeier and Marie Howland a review.

Coyne, R., Lamberton, D., Bruce, H., Strand, J.R., MacDougall, S., Ogden, M.R., Layton, S., Molnar, H., Wells, D., Chatwin, D., Wickramanayake, E., and **Boaden, C.**, 1995, Information Technology and Development (11 papers). *Development Bulletin* vol. 35 pp. 3–39.
This discussion, spread over 11 papers, questions the widely held assumption that improved communication systems and the free flow of information and knowledge carry positive benefits for developing countries. It is becoming increasingly apparent that information technologies do not necessarily support beneficial change, rather promote the disparity between the rich and the poor, and the developed and developing countries. Coyne argues that vast information of often conflicting nature

available on the Internet has led to scepticism about professional expertise and greater pressure on the individual to decide what to do. In the next paper, Lamberton considers the emergence of electronic colonialism because of inappropriate or incomplete information infrastructures. Bruce focuses on the considerable barriers many developing countries face because of their involvement with the internet. The dramatic impact of the new technologies on libraries and the ways in which large statistical data bases are stored, accessed and utilized is discussed by Chatwin. The other papers examine the following; telecommunications and economic development (Strand); Pacific Islands and information technology (Ogden); the CocoNet Wireless which operates between the Pacific Islands (Layton); issues relating to the development of communications in the South Pacific; the utilization of computers by NGOs in development programmes (Wells); and, the use of computers in rural development planning in Thailand (Wickramanayake).

Cyranek, Gunther, and **Bhatnagar, Subhash**, 1992, *Technology Transfer for Development: The Prospects and Limits of Information Technology*, Tata McGraw-Hill, New Delhi.

Dutta, S., 1997, Role of Women in Rural Energy Programmes: Issues, Problems and Opportunities. *Energia-News (Netherlands)*, no. 4, pp. 11–14.
Available : Databases through 'Webspirs'
Accession Number: 109564
In the rural areas of India, women have traditionally shouldered the responsibility of managing the domestic energy requirements for their families. However, they have no role in the management and control of resources. In government-initiated programmes in the rural energy and environment sectors, there are few mechanisms to incorporate a meaningful role for women in project planning and implementation. Lack of involvement of women at all stages in the project cycle has been identified as one of the major causes of the limited sustainability of projects. A number of factors act as barriers to the effective participation of women in rural energy dissemination programmes. These include traditional decision making role of the male in society; the level of economic independence; and education constraints leading to lack of access to information, skills and technical expertise.

Foley, 1995, Photo Voltaic Applications for Rural Areas of the Developing World, World Bank Technical Paper 304, Washington D.C., IDRD/The World Bank, p. 79.

Grimes, Seamus, 1992, Exploiting Information and Communication Technologies for Rural Development. *Journal of Rural Studies*, 8(3), pp. 269–78.

Hallows, Jolyon E., 1997, *Information Systems Project Management: How to Deliver Function and Value in Information Technology Projects*.

Hanna, Nagy, 1994, *Exploiting Information Technology for Development—A Case Study of India*. World Bank, Washington D.C.

Hanna, Nagy, Guy Ken, and **Arnold, Erik**, 1995, The Diffusion of Information Technology—Experience of Industrial Countries and Lessons for Developing Countries, World Bank Discussion Paper 281, Washington D.C., IDRB/World Bank, p. 207. This study reports on the experience of Canada, Germany, Ireland, the Netherlands, Sweden, the United Kingdom, the United States, and Japan in designing, implementing and adapting information technology (IT) diffusion programmes in the 1990s. The study examines the determinants of effective IT diffusion and analyzes national IT policy portfolios to draw lessons and trends. Programmes should consider technology life cycles, the business needs of potential users, their technological sophistication, and their current exposure to international best practices. The study concludes by suggesting roles for governments, private sector, and aid agencies to accelerate the benefits of IT diffusion for development.

Hawkins, J., Valantin, R.(eds), *Development and the Information Age: Four Global Scenarios for the Future of Information and Communication Technology*, International Development Research Centre (IDRC) Ottawa, Canada.
Four scenarios of potential development within information and communication technology (ICT) are presented. These were conceived through a workshop held in 1996 by the United Nations Commission on Science and Technology for Development. The report starts with the raw material for the topic: development issues, ICT issues, and ICTs and development. It then describes the two critical uncertainties that cloud the future of ICTs and development: the global system and national policies. On the basis of the analysis and the uncertainties, it presents the four scenarios that were developed. The conclusions are drawn on the basis of the issues covered.

Hickson, B., 1996, Revitalising Rural Communities through Telexchanges, in, D. Sless (ed.) *The Informationless Society*, Communication Research Institute of Australia, Canberra.

Horejs, I., 1996, *IT in Rural Development Planning: The Case of Nicaragua*. Roche E.M., and Blaine M.J. (eds) Future Roles of Information Technology in Rural Development. Avebury Aldershot, UK 1996, pp. 209–28.
This paper analyzes the role of information technology in rural development planning. The first section introduces the theoretical debate about regional planning for rural development and the role of information technology. Viewing rural development as a process of socio-economic change aimed at reducing poverty and inequalities among the population of rural areas, regional development planning is defined as a decentralized, participatory decision making process. The main potential benefit of information technology is its potential to enable not only better informed decision making but also organizational change and improved working procedures. The second section contains description and analysis of the experience of establishing a computer supported information system as part of a regional planning system for rural development in a northern Nicaraguan region. The final section employs this case to draw some general lessons about IS development and design and to identify some critical factors concerning implementation.

Hudson, Heather E., 1995, Economic and Social Benefits of Rural Telecommunications, A Report to the World Bank. World Bank, Washington D.C.

Kamaluddin, S., 1997, Calling Countryfolk. *Far Eastern Economic Review [FER]* 160(17) p. 79.
Access No: 01411408 ProQuest ABI/INFORM (R) Global
Grameen Telecom aims at revolutionizing communications, and consequently the

economic development of rural Bangladesh. Grameen is betting that thousands of people will sign up for low-priced services from Grameen Phone, a joint venture cellular-phone network operator.

Kayani Rogati, and **Dymond Andrew**, 1997, Options for Rural Telecommunications Development, World Bank Technical Paper 359, Washington D.C. The World Bank, p. 118.

This technical report provides a comprehensive analysis of the technical and financial parameters that have to be considered in formulating policies to reduce the disparities between urban and rural telecommunications services. It addresses the following fundamental issues regarding commercial provision of rural telecommunications services: (*a*) the implications of the various sector reform models on rural telecommunications development; (*b*) technology and cost trends; (*c*) pricing and tariff setting options; (*d*) commercial viability and revenue generation potential; and (*e*) funding issues. Useful case study data was collected from more than 26 developing countries. The report also presents an array of options for commerical operation and challenges the general perception that rural telecommunications services are unprofitable. Services can be economically delivered to rural areas at affordable prices while at the same time providing reasonable financial returns to investors.

Klitgaard, Robert, 1991, *Adjusting to Reality: Beyond 'State vs Market' in Economic Development*. An International Centre for Economic Growth Publication, ICS Press.

In the developing world, corrupt governments, ethnic strife, and weak markets are the ground reality. How can governments shift from controlling economic development to facilitating it? What can be done to bridge economic and educational gaps among ethnic groups? How can the market place be made to serve the poor as well as the advantaged. In a lively and insightful fashion, Robert Klitgaard provides new and practical answers to these questions.

Kohli, Vanita, 1999, Getting Wired, the Warana Way. *Business World*, February 22–March 6, pp. 72–73.

The recently launched Warana Wired Village Project covering 70 villages around the river Warana in Maharashtra is described. The existing cooperative structure has been used in concert with state of the art infrastructure (notably high speed VSATs) to allow Internet access to existing cooperative societies. The project aims to provide agricultural, medical, and education information to villagers by establishing networked 'facilitation booths' in the villages.

Subramanyan, L., 1999, Unsung Heroes. *Voice and Data*, January 1.

Lee, Jeanne, 1998, Satellite Phone Service Takes Off in Indonesia. *Fortune* [FOR] 137(5) March 16, p. 154; European 76

Access No: 01588390 ProQuest ABI/INFORM (R) Global

Pasifik Satelit Nusantara installed about 2,000 satellite phones in Indonesian villages in 1997. The system consists of a satellite disk, a terminal box, and a telephone handset. The gear can be hooked up in an hour, and the calls are cheap. Telcos lease time on satellites owned by the likes of Loral and Hughes. Nusantara makes a profit only if the phones are used more than 90 minutes a day.

Lown, B., Bukachi, F., and **Xavier, R.,** 1998, Health Information in the Developing World. *Lancet* (British edition) 352 (SUPPII), pp. 34–38.
An evaluation is made of the impact of information on the health sector, focusing particularly on the developing world. The paper discusses the development of electronic sources of information, although agrees that it creates a divide between those who have access to the technology, and those who do not. Issues discussed are: the Internet; medical information for health transition; and SatelLife, a low-earth-orbit satellite which increases access to HealthNet for areas with poor telecommunications infrastructures.

Machlis, Sharon, 1997, Web Tool Helps Fight World Poverty,. *Computerworld* [COW] 31(28), July 14, pp. 37–38.
Access No: 01466895 ProQuest ABI/INFORM (R) Global
The United Nations' International Fund for Agricultural Development's (IFAD) office of evaluation and studies developed a computerized knowledge base culled from 461 projects undertaken since 1978. Initially, the data resided on an internal network. A revised version is now available on the world wide web. IFAD aims at becoming a knowledge centre on fighting rural poverty. The internal network has already helped similar projects in Ghana, India and Nicaragua to learn from each other, as experiences help formulate suggestions for what to do—and what not to do—when spending money on agricultural projects.

Mansell, Robin, and **Wehn, Uta** (eds), 1998, *Knowledge Societies: Information Technology for Sustainable Development.* United Nations Commission for Science and Technology for Development, Oxford University Press.

Mchombu, K., 1995, Impact of Information on Rural Development. *Making a Difference,* IDRC, Ottawa.

McKinsey et al., 1995 Closing the Global Communications Gap: An assessment of WorldTel's Feasibility to Commercially Narrow the North-South Gap in Telecommunications and Information Infrastructure (mimeo).

Mehta, Dewang, 1999, Stepping on the information highway. *The Financial Express,* Mumbai. February 26.
The growing awareness of the Internet in rural India is explored by analyzing the current policy scenario governing the Internet and the current business dynamics in the Internet industry.

Mitter, S., and **Rowbotham, S.,** 1995, *Women Encounter Technology: Changing Patterns of Employment in the Third World,* Routledge London, UK.
The papers in this book form a contribution towards the literature of women's studies and of development economics. They document the impact of information technology on the working lives of women in developing countries. Although presenting empirical observations, the papers also raise questions of women's autonomy and agency and try to articulate women's needs and demands. Challenges that women face in adjusting to the demands of information technology are the focal points of the essays; yet women's response and organizing strategies when confronted with such challenges equally permeate the arguments and analyses. They highlight the roles that family, ideology, state policies, and trade union structures play in distributing IT-related employment between women and men. The

papers present case studies of textile production in Brazil and Argentina; changes in textiles and the implications for Asian women; women's employment in manufacturing in eastern Europe, the case of Slovenia; the Canadian garment industry in transition; women's employment in India's banking sector; the telecommunications industry in Malaysia; software programming in Brazil; the electronics industry in Calcutta; information technology in sub-Saharan Africa; and the Tanzanian Media Women's Association.

Mukund, Padmanabhan, 1999, Andhra Pradesh IT-for-people initiative. *The Hindu*, January 6.

The Andhra Pradesh government's Computer-aided Administration of Registration Department (CARD) project is directed at altering the antiquated procedures that governed the land registration and transfer system, which not only included the labourious copying and indexing of documents but also their unscientific space consuming preservation in ill-maintained back-rooms. The project is an effort to use IT to smoothen the interface between citizens and the government.

Nusantara Communications, Inc., web site address: http://www.nci-arts.com

Nusantara Communications, Inc. has developed the Advanced Rural Telephone System, a wireless telephone standard offering an integrated network solution for rural telephony that lies between point-to-multipoint (PMP), trunk radio, and wireless local loop technologies. Because of its integrated and distributed switching capability, ARTS provides a complete and cost-effective local network infrastructure for remote locations based on radio communications. Designed specifically to meet rural network requirements, the Advanced Rural Telephone System can interface directly with the public switched telephone network for national and international telephone calls and also operate as a stand-alone wireless system, serving essential services as a miniature central office for telephone calls within the rural cell area.

Odera-Straub, Mayuri, Okot-Uma, Rogers, and **Cyranek, Gunther**, 1995, (eds) *Information Technology and Globalization: Implications for Developing Countries*. Commonwealth Secretariat, London.

This publication looks at the role of information technology (IT) in the globalization process and its implications on developing countries (DCs). Ten articles address various issues related to: the impact of IT on MNCs and TNCs; the implications of virtual organizations on workers; the illusion created by a global network as a socially productive technology; the domination of the developed world in the globalization process; globalization leading to modernization; the globalization of economies; opportunities for DCs in the global process; IT infrastructures; policies and plans influencing globalization.

Richardson, Don, 1997, The Internet and Rural Development: Opportunities for Forestry. Department of Rural Extension Studies, University of Guelph, Canada. Conference Title: Special issue: Computers and Forestry. *Unasylva* (English edition), 48(189), pp. 3–9.

The potential of use of the Internet with regard to forestry and rural development is discussed.

Richardson, Don, 1997, *The Internet and Rural and Agricultural Development: An Integrated Approach*, Food and Agriculture Organization of the United Nations, Rome.

Roche, E. M., and **Blaine, M.J.** (eds), 1996, *Information Technology, Development and Policy: Theoretical Perspectives and Practical Challenges*. International Development Research Centre (IDRC) Ottawa, Canada.

Sangwan, Soni, 1999, Taking Information Technology to the Doorstep of Those in Need. *The Hindustan Times*, March 26.
Knowledge system launched by M. S. Swaminathan makes information available to the very people who need it and benefit from it the most.

Sharma, Motilal, 1996, Communications Technologies in Open and Distance Learning in Asia: The Experience of the Asian Development Bank. Keynote address presented at the Conference on Educational Technology 2000 (Singapore, August 15–17.
Available : Databases through 'Webspirs'
Accession Number: ED404546
In view of financial constraints, large numbers of students to be educated, and rapid changes in information and communication and information technology, open learning (OL) and distance education (DE) systems are being established at an unprecedented rate in almost all developing countries of the Asian and Pacific region. Modern communications, computer-aided programmes, and DE and OL systems should be applied vigorously to four areas: reduction of poverty, especially among rural populations; enlargement of human development in all aspects of physical, intellectual, and spiritual areas; improvement of women's status; and contribution to national peace and elimination of violence and terrorism. DE and OL help improve the quality of information and reduce the information gap. The core strength of DE is that it can globalize the education system by bringing in the best available teachers and experts to any corner of the world to provide the latest information with the help of communication technology.

Talero, E., and **Gaudette, P.**, 1996, Harnessing Information for Development: Proposal for a World Bank Strategy, World Bank Discussion Paper 313.

Talmor, Gidi, and **Meirzon, Tal**, 1998, Rural Telephony Comes into its Own. *Satellite Communications* [SAC], 22(10), pp. 53–56
Access No: 01708196 ProQuest ABI/INFORM (R) Global
Rural telephony has been on the agenda of governments and international organizations for years. Cost is the biggest hurdle. Very Small Aperture Terminal (VSAT) solutions allow for reliable data, voice and video communications using small satellite antennas. VSAT vendors have succeeded in steadily lowering the price of the terminals while increasing their features and functionality. The idea is to give rural subscribers what they need, and not make them pay for what they do not need. Smaller rural populations may be content with even one or two telephone lines in their village. The risk of investment in an unproven rural area is overcome with VSAT technology. The first line in a village can be installed for a minimal investment. This line becomes profitable soon after deployment and, as traffic increases, the number of channels can be increased at little marginal cost.

The Hindu, 1999, Information Technology will Make Knowledge Accessible to Villagers, January 6.

The objective of a pilot project launched by the M. S. Swaminathan Research Foundation, Chennai, is to make adequate knowledge available to the villagers to ensure sustainable food security.

The Hindu, 1999, Move to Computerize Panchayats in Rajasthan, January 28.

The chief minister of Rajasthan, a state in north-western India, has said that his state will invest in creating an IT network to connect all the village administrations in the state capital for improving the quality of service offered to the citizens.

Wellenius, B., 1997, Extending Telecommunications Service to Rural Areas—The Chilean Experience. World Bank Industry and Energy Department Viewpoint, Note No. 105. 1997.

Chile has provided a model of government intervention to move toward the goal of wider access. To increase rural and low-income access, the government set up a limited life Telecommunications Development Fund. The fund provides lump sum subsidies for public telephone provision in localities where the social net present value of telephones per unit of subsidy has been estimated to be at a maximum. After a first round of competitive bidding in 1995–96, the fund had to commit only 48 per cent of its budget to attract private investors for 42 out of 46 chosen projects. These projects connected over 1,000 localities at a total cost to the fund of just $2.1 million (Rs 9 crores approx.). The fund's minimal public investment leveraged private investment of about $40 million (Rs 172 crores).

Zajtchuk, Russ, Edward, Mozley Roche, and **Michael, James Blaine** (eds), 1996, *Information Technology, Development, and Policy: Theoretical Perspectives and Practical Challenges*. Aldershot, Hants, England; Brookfield, Vt.: Avebury.

Zhang QiaoQiao, and **Cheng XiaoLan**, 1996, Provision of Information to the Rural Communities in China, in, Powell, A. P.(ed.) *Quarterly Bulletin of IAALD*, 41(1), pp. 109–16.

Efficient information dissemination and services for rural communities in China will rely largely on the introduction of effective channels of communication and modern information technology. This technology should include live demonstrations of plots or farms experimenting with new techniques and varieties, audio, visual and satellite-transmitted information, multimedia, interactive and expert information systems, and on the proactive provision of targeted, specialized and digested information via consultancy and question–answer services. The high priority given by the government to sustainable agriculture and the rapidly improving price/performance of electronic publishing and telecommunications in China should encourage such efficient information dissemination and services to rural communities.

Zijp, Willem, 1994, *Future Roles of Information Technology in Rural Development, Agriculture and Natural Resources Department*, World Bank, March.

About the Editors and Contributors

Editors

Subhash Bhatnagar is CMC Professor of IT at the Indian Institute of Management, (IIM), Ahmedabad, and is currently coordinating a CIDA sponsored Telecom Policy Research Centre at the IIM in collaboration with McGill University. He is also coordinating a centre for electronic governance established at IIM with the support of the IT industry. Prof. Bhatnagar is Founder Chairman of the IFIP working group on Social Implications of Computers in Developing Countries and the editor of its newsletter on *Information Technology in Developing Countries*. He has published several books and papers, and has lectured in 40 countries.
e-mail: subhash@iimahd.ernet.in

Robert Schware is a Senior Informatics Specialist in the Global Information and Communications Technology Department of the World Bank, Washington, D.C., where he manages informatics portfolios consisting of projects to develop information infrastructure, computer literacy, and various applications of ICT for government and rural development in Turkey, Indonesia and India, among other countries. Dr Schware recently spent a year as Visiting Professor at the Indian Institute of Management, Ahmedabad, while currently on a World Bank sponsored External Development Program Assignment.
e-mail: rschware@worldbank.org

Contributors

B.S. Bhatia is Director of the Distant Education Communications Unit at the Indian Space Research Organization.
e-mail: bsbhatia@yahoo.com

Rupak Chakravarty is Manager of Sector Planning and Systems at the National Dairy Development Board.
e-mail: rupak@anand.nddb.ernet.in

Santosh Choubey is Director of the All India Society for Electronics and Computer Technology.

Mike Graves is Chief Technology Officer, Concept Labs, California.
e-mail: mgraves@conceptlabs.net

Anil K. Gupta is a Professor at the Indian Institute of Management, Ahmedabad, and Coordinator of the Society for Research and Initiatives for Sustainable Technologies and Institutions (SRISTI).
e-mail: anilg@iimahd.ernet.in

Raj Gupta is Regional Director (Central and Eastern Asia) at Inmarsat.
e-mail: rkgupta@del1.vsnl.net.in

Brij Kothari is a Professor at the Indian Institute of Management, Ahmedabad.
e-mail: brij@iimahd.ernet.in

Asok Kumar has been Project Director of the Computerization of Mandal Revenue Offices Project, Government of Andhra Pradesh.
e-mail: asokg@ap.nic.in

Raja Mitra is an Economist at the World Bank.
e-mail: rmmitra@hotmail.com

Reema Nanavati is Director of Rural Development at SEWA (Self Employed Women's Association).
e-mail: bdmsa@ad1.vsnl.net.in

Kirit Patel is Associate Editor of the Honey Bee Network.
e-mail: honeybee@iimahd.ernet.in

Bhushan Punani is Executive Director of the Blind People's Association.
e-mail: blinab@ad1.vsnl.net.in

Late Major Ramakrishnan was Country Manager for Health, CMC Ltd.
e-mail: major@cmcdak.cmc.stph.net

Naresh Kumar Reddy is a Senior Project Manager, R&D, at CMC Ltd.
e-mail: naresh@cmcltd.com

J. Satyanarayana is Secretary of Information Technology, Government of Andhra Pradesh.

Joe Takeda is a Lecturer at Kwansei Gakuin University, Nishinomiya, Japan.
e-mail: jotakeda@yahoo.com

Krishna S. Vatsa is Deputy Secretary, Government of Maharashtra.
e-mail: vatsa@bom5.vsnl.net.in

N. Vijayaditya is Deputy Director General of the National Informatics Centre.
e-mail: drnv@hub.nic.in

Index